PAINT FOR YOURSELF

By Christian Title

I0490296

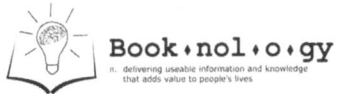

A BUSINESS & EDUCATIONAL IMPRINT FROM ADDUCENT
WWW.ADDUCENTINC.COM

TITLES DISTRIBUTED IN
NORTH AMERICA
UNITED KINGDOM
WESTERN EUROPE
SOUTH AMERICA
AUSTRALIA
CHINA
INDIA

PAINT FOR YOURSELF

By Christian Title

PAINT FOR YOURSELF
Christian Title

ISBN 9781937592783

Published by Booknology (a business and educational imprint from Adducent)
Jacksonville, Florida
www.AdducentInc.com

All statements of fact, opinion, or analysis expressed are those of the author and do not reflect the official positions or views of the publisher. Nothing in the contents should be construed as asserting or implying authentication of information or endorsement of the author's views. This book and subjects discussed herein are designed to provide the author's opinion about the subject matter covered and is for informational purposes only.

TABLE OF CONTENTS

DEDICATION

To my wife of fifty years who has shared my visions and dreams, and my lifelong friend, artist John Powell who has followed his own path and found the magic

ACKNOWLEDGMENTS

To the teachers who give so much and guide the young, who so often sacrifice their own ambitions

INTRODUCTION

During my long career as an exhibiting artist, I have been exposed to a continued misconception of motivations and reasons for painting. Most of the people that express the desire to pursue art are led on a path of faulty thinking. They join a class and are shown the rudiments of applying paint to canvas. The base of this criteria is to reproduce something, typically a painting or a photograph. Their motivation becomes the desire to please others and to receive some kind of praise for their efforts. This superficial approach will manifest in mediocre work, which yields few personal rewards. The vast majority of people lose interest and soon the quest is abandoned. Why? Because it is not rewarding and it isn't fun!

What should the motivation be?

First, let's examine the nature of art itself. Why should we draw, or put paint to canvas? To record our personal feelings. The language for this recording is shapes, colors, and texture. Art is not about reproduction, Art is about creativity and imagination. We ask how to best express these emotions and how we can make it a joy.

What I have proposed in this book is a method that will bring you pleasure. It will be enjoyable, and exciting. Over an extended period, it will bring deep satisfaction and an understanding of yourself that will fill your life with the magic of creativity. This approach will foster new ideas and inspire you to more ambitious endeavors, and in the end, you will produce a level of individual work that is unique.

The primary barrier to this path will be the isolation, but you must accept and embrace that--in a way, it is an avenue of psychological joys and adjustments—and as you become the artist within, you will gain stature and strength. You will experience a level of understanding and happiness that grows and makes life itself the objective.

"Every child is an artist. The problem is how to remain an artist once we grow up." --Pablo Picasso

Observe the art of a young child, four or five years old. If given the material and left to their own devices, they will occupy themselves for long periods. Over time, if the adults do not impose influence, they will take a path that is very much like what I propose. But, they must not be directed in any manner whatsoever and will begin to be more involved, and the images will manifest with greater clarity. They will create their own sophistication and style.

It is interesting to note that Pablo Picasso was not a renowned collector of his contemporaries, even though they became recognized as some of the most influential artists in history. When he died, it was learned he was an avid collector of drawings and paintings by children.

Give some thought to the child's desires and motivation. Not trying to please others, they are likely just making something they find rewarding. The most interesting part is how they grow without outside direction.

I recall one particular case vividly, that of a friend when I was quite young. His daughter was given paper, paint, crayons, pencils, and clay for molding things, with only the natural desire she had because she watched her father paint in his studio. I was amazed at the long hours she could spend pursuing any number of projects which were of her own making. Over the years I had many conversations with her father about his philosophy of letting her grow in her own direction. When she was about eight years old, she was doing wonderful, magical designs that were uniquely her own. Her father had ceased easel painting and had gone to work for the movie studios painting backgrounds. I lost track of them, but I never forgot how impressed I was with the great individuality and charm of her creations.

* * *

What I present is the path for an individual that has not pursued art seriously as a career and not taken any formal training. It is for those who wish to occupy their time with something exciting and rewarding. I will guide you into a personal realm of imagination, fantasy, creativity, and pride. But I also feel the experienced professional can benefit as I know how difficult it was for me to abandon the formal approach to art for the magical. I have been repetitious in this book and pursue the subject from many aspects to drive home the ideas that I wish to bestow.

THE SOCIAL ASPECTS OF ART

The social side of art is what is familiar to most of us. The exchange of creative ideas, methods of work, the public exhibitions and the social relationships built around the camaraderie of mutual interest. The ideas and the sharing of interest in the art world, pursued by the majority of those who wish to be in what they perceive as the mainstream, is simplistic understanding. The profound side of this equation is quite a different story. The popular and public part of the art world is interesting and has many facets of participation. To immerse yourself in this realm is rewarding on a different level than the discovery process in finding one's own internal archive. It is simpler, more direct, and easily manipulated for pleasure and rewards. But, it does not hold the permanent passion and understanding that can be achieved through the intuitive personal pursuit into one's own psyche. There is a level of elation and lasting joy associated with this private sphere of consciousness.

In this book, I pursue the personal and intuitive realm of the imagination and creative process. Carl Jung said, "Man can achieve wholeness only through dreams and their symbols. Every dream is a direct personal and meaningful communication to the dreamer that uses the symbols common to all mankind. But uses them always in an entirely individual way, which can be interpreted only by a unique key."

My life in art began when I was eight years old. So, I have been intently interested in the inspiration, execution and visual pleasures, which have been my joy, for a lifetime. I majored in art in high school and was fortunate to have a teacher who mentored and encouraged me to pursue it with great passion. I received my Bachelor of Arts degree from Woodbury University. My master's degree from the famous Beaux-Arts Académie in Paris, and my doctorate from the Sorbonne University. I did further post-graduate work at the Bella Institute in Rome, Heidelberg University in Germany and Edinburgh University in Scotland. I was fortunate to have studied and worked with such greats as Oskar Kokoschka, Andre Lhote, Fernand Leger, and Pierre-Jerome. I have had meetings and conversations with artists such as Francis Bacon, Juan Miro, and many accomplished artists from many countries. I became a very successful art dealer, and that led to a thorough understanding of the exhibiting and commercial aspects of the art world. In that seventy years of an all-consuming career as artist and art dealer, I gained a perspective that I feel can benefit anyone with the passion for painting, or to just absorb and appreciate this enjoyable creative process.

If we create the environment of mind and adhere to the principals of our private world, that world will mold itself into the images transformed of a single-minded passion. There is a manifesto silently declared by the techno-futurist element and its influence on our children. The need is that it must be humanized into sensual imagery. This objective has not found a champion to synthesize it meaningfully into a realm of acceptance in today's art atmosphere. There is within it a seductive challenge that could manifest in a cubistic sensual classicism. We need a leader with a goal, not to copy, but to create a new style and return to an elegance of line and color. Abandoning the current forces to complete the destruction of painting as pronounced in the history of art.

PROLOGUE
The Stew of Life

Life is really like a stew. There is the mixture of meat, potatoes, and vegetables, and when you cook it all up, it is nourishing but bland. It is only when you add the seasonings: salt, pepper, garlic, ginger, thyme, and the spices that create a taste that one would describe as delicious.

What makes life nourishing? Health, love, comfort, work, and play. What makes it delicious? Travel, intellect, friendship, wealth. What are the ingredients that make it exquisite? Art, Music, and Literature! Most people don't understand the primary drives and inspirational rewards that come from these components. My subject is art, and I can only explain it by telling the history of how it developed within me.

When I was only two or three years old, my father tucked us in bed at night and told my brother and me wonderful imaginative stories. It was a time of heroes, villains, monsters, werewolves, mummies, of outer spaces and magical worlds. My mother would scold him for getting us too riled up to sleep. It did just that, but only for a short period before I entered the world of dreams. I would lie there afterward and compose my own endings, characters and wild additions to the script. These flights of imagination were the foundation of my creativity. I remember going to the beach in Santa Monica one day. My brother and I started to build sand castles close to the water where the sand was moist and would be pliable enough to hold together. My brother made an island with a moat around it and buildings in the middle, He was a year and a half older and more ambitious in his project. I leveled out a flat plain and made a series of round bumps on the surface.

My brother asked me, "What is that?"

"It's the Bumpy people. They're like Turtles. They walk around, and when they sleep or are scared, they plunk down on the ground and hide."

Because I took a lot of flak for the Bumpy people, I made up stories about their society and how eventually they would control the world. The tide came in, and the castle and the Bumpy people were washed away. That didn't matter, it was the imagination and execution that was the fulfilling aspect of the endeavor. Not the finished product. So, I learned that the creative process and the time spent in the making of the reality was the essential part of the equation. As I say many times to people who express the desire to paint, it doesn't matter if you are accomplished, but only if you have the imagination to make something that is personal and from your own mind. The creative process is the fulfilling part.

Let's look at the historical background of the art world, in a nutshell, so to speak.

Primitive man expressed himself in cave drawings to record his understanding of his world and to document his hunting prowess. The first cultures recorded events this way because there was no written language to communicate their accomplishments or deeds. Art progressed until the skill to reproduce was refined enough to make a complete statement. That eventually lead to the pigments and paints and the reproductive quality that could be almost photographic. When the great masters developed their talents to the point of a realistic understanding of the portrayal, they began to illustrate the fables and biblical inspirations beyond the illustrative, and the element of the narrative was infused. The interpretation of descriptive visions were the first elements of real creativity.

The creative process continued to grow to a point where the image was solely of the artist's mind. In photography, we look at pictures that are familiar, but often are inspirational in their content. Various forms of the photographic skill have created images that are abstract. But the process by the photographer remains technical, and it is his skill at numerous techniques that compose an image of artistic value. It is less of the emotional and spontaneous response to his imagination. An exquisite painting is one that encompasses the full creative understanding of line and color, expressed clearly from that unknown world of the artist's mind. The realm of the representational is abandoned for the imagery of the magical.

CHAPTER ONE
Aspects of the Creative Mind

In my years of exposure to some great talents in music, art, literature, and science, I have drawn certain parallels in their personalities and mannerisms. There is primarily, beneath the surface, a mental partition that is not noticeable with casual contact. But the emotionally detached element becomes evident when a more intimate association is developed. As has been observed by many psychologists and writers, this inward direction is conducive to the advanced creative process.

It is my opinion that many are driven by the fear of loving and commitment A trait often observed is a fiery reaction to the contrary views of others. The anxiety builds and they—the human—withdraws to the sanctity of their private thoughts. They would rather deal with the frustration of isolation than to hear something that they deem as an unreasonable conclusion.

There is a calm that is the reward of isolation. It is the arena for pure thought and manifests in work of significance. The dynamics of creation are the links to aesthetic pleasure. There are fear and an accomplishment in that need. Excluding others will, over time, help develop significant breakthroughs which then lead to more isolation and more eccentric behavior. Being aware of these tendencies I have had fears, and strive to communicate on a reasonable level with friends. Sometimes it is difficult to accept that they are not tuned in to anything that I value. They often are not well read, have no knowledge or interest in art, and enjoy music on a superficial level. But, on the other hand, they are often very successful in business, law, medicine or other professions. I try to have an interest in these activities, and not escape into my personal world.

When the individual finds his separate path into the world of imagination, it is hard to turn back and steal the time for other pursuits. I treasure my creative time, but age and energy are the enemies. Loved ones do not grasp the concept that you are not ignoring them or that you don't have an agenda that excludes them, or that you are not purposely inattentive to their needs.

My mother called me the 'Dreamer' when I was a boy. I remember it was more fun to venture into my fantasies, then to listen to the boring teachers and their mundane subjects. I would rather think about Buck Rogers and the evil Red Dragon

So, here I am eighty-five years old, still walking the tightrope between my precious private world and the civilization that embraces me.

BEGINNING

In 2008, I had a narrow escape from some of the realities I have never faced. I have always taken my health for granted, and indeed I have enjoyed more than seven decades of good health and strength. After a heart attack and a triple bypass surgery, with significant complications, I lay frustrated and weak in the hospital. More than anything, though my body was aching and my clarity of thought came and went like the tides of the sea. My mind was active, but the means of expression and energy to do so were limited. I found myself thinking about the things that I would pass on, about my passions and the advice I would give to others about what I have learned in a long and eventful life, the things that I am so sure of.

I have spent most of my life drawing, painting, observing, studying art history, dealing in art, and dealing with artists AND am often asked about pursuing painting. The advice I would give is as follows.

To the young who wish to pursue a career in art. Start with a pencil, draw cubes, spheres, statues, hands, and feet... anything and everything in sight. Look for the forms, study the light. Draw until it becomes second nature to have a pencil in your hand. When you feel comfortable and agile with graphite, it is time to move on to color.

Study the color wheel, know the spectrum intimately. Then progress from the drawing, pick up the brushes (only medium and large in the beginning). Attack the canvas with wild abandon, enjoy the magic of color. Make broad, quick landscapes, colorful heads and still life's. Think only of color and what pleases you. Bright yellow skies, red mountains, purple people, and an aggressive palette. Keep it broad, but as you progress, increase your contrasts, refine your composition, be conscious of the volumes so that it does not become static. Start to use smaller and less flexible brushes, refine into the broad approach canvas that you used previously, working while the surface remains wet. If necessary use oil as a medium to preserve the paint, so it does not dry quickly. Many lessons will be learned with this approach, to be free with your brush stroke, daring with your colors and bold in your choices.

Work in this manner until you can pull all the elements together, after which you can pursue painting in more of a dry method or any way that you wish because you have learned the significant aspects of a great artist: drawing, color, and freedom.

The above advice is for the young, those who have the time and patience to put the building blocks in place no matter how tedious, because theirs is the pursuit of long-term passion and satisfaction. But, I will speak now of the person over forty years old who wishes to pursue the arts as a hobby or partial profession. The mind needs relaxation and concentration that steers us away from the tensions of other stressful activities. Because the objective should be one of joy and a new passion that creates a new voyage of the mind. The end result is not something to worry about; it can be scraped off with a palette knife. Do not fear the stark white surface that seems so daunting, attack it with large or medium size brushes. The primary purpose is to have fun, accept the challenge and you will improve steadily with each canvas. More than anything, do not seek the approval of others. Find areas in your own work that are pleasing to you, expand on these. Study the work of famous artists, both traditional and abstract. Try to see and feel the passion of the artist. Do not base your understanding of photographic imagery. Remember that everyone looks, but few really see. Understanding what you see, regarding form, volume and color are the keys.

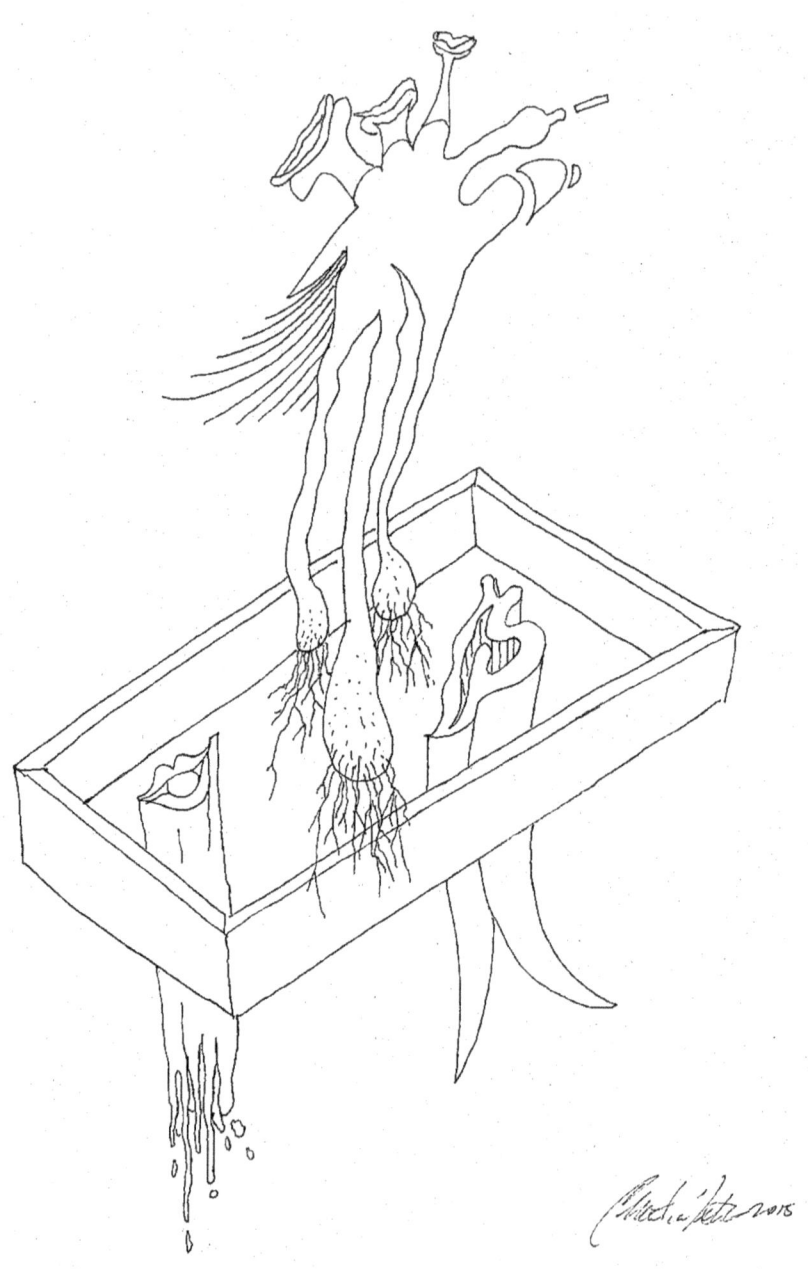

CHAPTER TWO
Personal Philosophies

I relate the following as it encompasses the typical storyline of nearly all the artists I have known, with a few exceptions which I will also cover. The analysis of these artists, writers, and musicians described, is absent of the deficiencies that were not apparent to me at the time. If I had the knowledge then that I have today, I could have been of a much higher benefit to them.

Walter graduated from Woodbury University with me and received his B.A. He was a competent artist but with limited visual understanding. We traveled with two other artists who had graduated with us and enrolled in either the Beaux-Arts Academy or the Julian Academy in Paris. Walter was a hard worker and pursued his art with diligence. He painted the models and still life's that were set up each week at the Julian Academy. Over the years, we had many conversations about our work and dreams. So, I feel I had a real understanding of his goals. He mainly wanted to be a fine technician and produce beautiful landscapes and still life's that would sell so he could make a living as an artist.

Frank, one of the other artists of our group, had the most imagination and a wild sense of humor. His skill at sketching and characterizations were some of the best I have ever known. He loved life and Paris, and spent too much time pursuing the girls, and just socializing and hanging out in the cafes. He never reached any level of fine painting. Which in my mind was a great tragedy. His incredible interpretations of the models at school, people in the nightclubs, cafe scenes and the spirit and comedy of life was a natural talent which could have paved the way to realms that I can only suppose.

Frank and I shared an apartment for two years, and I admired his 'come what may' philosophy. He had such fun and enjoyment when he expressed himself with his wild machinations. Over time he learned to be a very competent painter, but could never translate his drawing ability and imagination to the canvas. Even in conversations of his work, he spoke with great enthusiasm and joy when discussing his drawings, but a melancholy look accompanied any discussions of painting. He tried many times to paint one of his drawings of cafe's or nightclub scenes, but he was defeated by color. He did not have the same daring, adventurous spirit when it came to color. I was unable at that time to analyze the problem, and he became discouraged and never fought his way through his dilemma. Had I known what I know today, he would have made the translation slowly and methodically until he had the same prowess in color. His work could have been spectacular. All the necessary elements were there, but the work ethic and the bulldog tenacity was not. Walter, on the other hand, became good at drawing and competent with color, but his work was never inspired, nor did he ever gain the kind of self-confidence and joy that was possible.

Jack was the fourth member of our group. He was very much like Walter in that he had little imagination and mental energy to experiment and enjoy every facet of his quest. Jack left Paris for a year and studied at the Fine Arts Academy of Copenhagen and when he returned to Paris, was truly a superb painter. He did beautiful portraits and landscapes. But, they were not anything more than the competent work being done by many of the graduate artists that surrounded us.

I was very young and my ambition to be a great artist lacked the overall comprehension of the scope involved. I was the best artist of the group because I had started when very young and achieved great skill in drawing. My drawing skills had been compared by many to the masters, and everyone raved about my work. But I had only a basic understanding of painting and failed to grasp the real essentials of what being an artist should be. I worked very hard at the Beaux-Arts Academy and pursued my academics at the Sorbonne University. I followed the Impressionists, the Fauves, the Cubists, the

Expressionists, and studied with Andre L'ote and Fernand Leger. These experiments changed my view and challenged me in every way. I continued to expand my knowledge and philosophies and to work hard at perfecting my skill. Slowly, I began to understand the elements that made this quest one of excitement and pleasure.

Walter returned to Los Angeles, he worked at several jobs while painting in his spare time. Eventually, he opened a small antique shop and studio in the beach town of El Segundo in the suburbs of Los Angeles. Walter sold antiques and taught little old ladies to paint still life's and landscapes. We remained friends all of our lives, and I know that he was content with his minor accomplishments. Walter died at seventy, as he was a heavy smoker. His wife told me after that he didn't understand my work and could not see why it was popular. Even in all the years, he pursued art, he never really grasped the most important aspects.

Frank returned home and got a job doing cartoons and characterizations for an advertising company that did the layouts for markets and merchandising. He advanced in this field and did some excellent newspaper political satires, that was much more in the realm of his talents. I lost track of Frank but when trying to contact him while writing my memoir, 'Climbed the Hill,' I learned of his death.

Jack returned and went to work in the construction industry. He eventually became a superintendent on some significant projects and only painted occasionally.

Each of my friends were victims of a conceptual fraud, perpetrated by the public in general, as people are unaware of the magic of creating. Imagination is the key to art and to life. Children understand that until they are immunized by their families, teachers and those who think they know the fundamentals of art. They are deceived into believing it is the traditional and representational that is fine art. But, they are mistaken, it is a realm beyond their understanding.

So, it was me that remained and spent a wondrous life with my art. In these pages, I will try to give you the reasons for painting and the challenge of life itself.

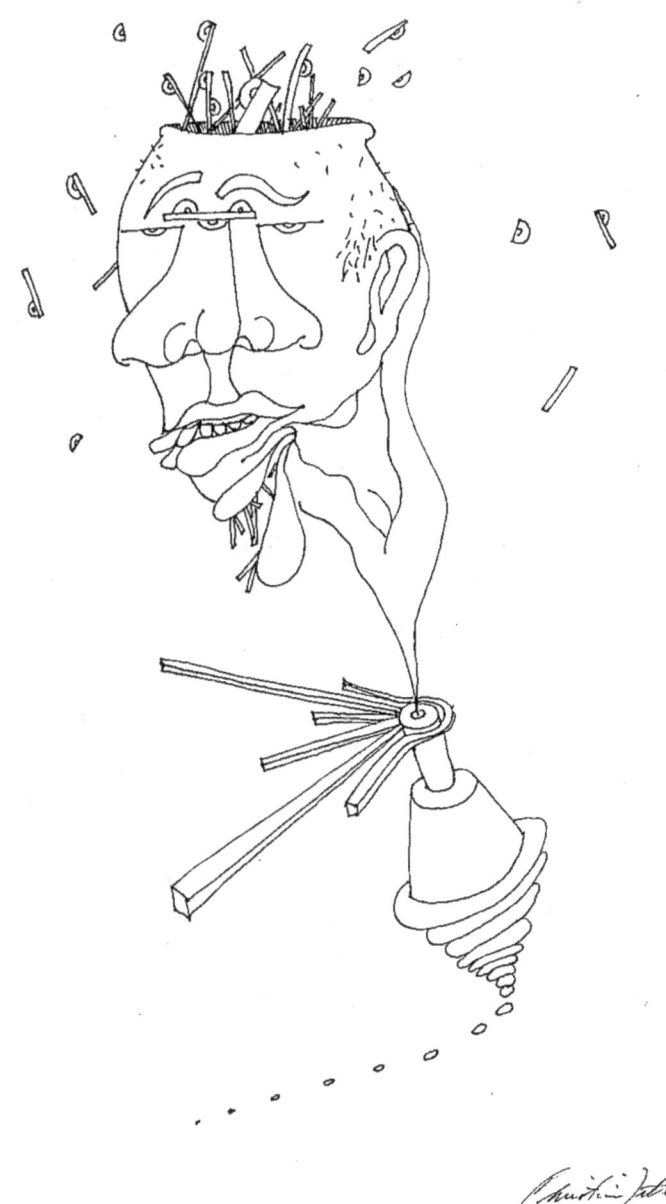

CHAPTER THREE
Barbara

Barbara is a friend of many years that expressed the desire to be a painter. And her story—I think—will be of interest to you. She was sixty-five years old and retired from a position that she had held for more than four decades. She grew up in that company and progressed through the ranks until she was a senior vice-president. She had devoted her life to her profession, and although successful financially had never married, had a few long-lasting relationships, was not necessarily compelled to make anything permanent with a partner. We had dated when we were young, and I had great respect for her abilities and ambitions. She had an excellent mind, was very attractive, and had a level of taste and presence that was admirable.

In our many conversations over the years, I understood that she had self- esteem, and confidence in nearly all areas of life. Her need for a man was minimal. She had many girlfriends that shared travel and various endeavors that were rewarding. What she needed at this juncture was something to take the place of her business life and give her an objective for the future. When Barbara was a young girl, she had pursued art in school superficially and had sustained interest in it over the years. And she had been attentive and supportive of my career. When she came to me and asked how she could get started, I told her of my philosophies and directives should she want to pursue art with the approach which I described. She said that the idea was appealing to her as it took away the fear of not being able to reproduce something representational without embarrassment.

Barbara was the kind of mind and personality that had great patience, but also a level of determination that was impressive. She went with me to a well-stocked art store, and we bought about six sketchbooks of various sizes. A box of a dozen fine-line waterproof ink pens. Bristle brushes from a quarter- inch up to a one-inch.

Several quarter-inch sable brushes and a half-dozen round pointed sable brushes. Two palette knives, one two-inch, and one four-inch. Six each of canvas boards: 12 inch x 16 inch, 16 inch x 20 inch, 20 inch x 24 inch, and 24 inch x 30 inch. She ordered a Hughes easel out of Florida, directly, as I had done considerable business with them. This easel is very stable, adjustable, and the best I have found. We ordered a complete selection of colors in three tube boxes, a paint box, odorless paint thinner, varnish, linseed oil and a two-inch sable varnish brush. We drove to a restaurant supply house and bought a large two-shelve cart used for moving bus trays in a restaurant. It had large wheels and was easily moved. The top was three feet long and two feet wide. She had a half-inch glass top made with a round edge that fit tightly into the three-quarter-inch bevel on the top of the cart. The weight of the glass gave it additional stability. The hardware store supplied several single-edge shaving blade holders, which are used to scrape the glass after the palette knife removes the bulk of the paint.

These are the kind of supplies I think is necessary if you are going to make the commitment. Barbara had a fully decorated bedroom which had a north facing window, but it was small, and the light was limited. She was a perfectionist and had the window replaced with a very large four by six-foot window, which converted the bedroom into a studio. She did all of this with the humor and lightness of someone who was on a lark and would just have a good time. We had many discussions about how she should start, and I encouraged her to concentrate on her drawing and not think about the painting for a few months. Over that time we met and had conversations many times, but I refused to see her work until she felt she had arrived at something that was a comprehensive foundation.

She had no input from anyone else and did not discuss her objectives with anyone. A year went by, and I was afraid that she was not progressing and would not have the fortitude to continue. But, I was mistaken. She had done hundreds of drawings of forms and shapes and things she found in an unbelievable number of books and photographs. She had installed an excellent drawing desk, bookshelves, and equipment to create an atmosphere of creativity. When she showed me her drawings, I could see that she had found a trend in the type of images that took her fancy.

When I asked her if she was ready to start painting, she said, "No, I'm having so much fun drawing that I just don't have the urge to paint. I know that I'm getting at something that is special and I'm so involved that I almost can't think of anything else. I was never in my life so inspired and excited as I am about where I'm going. When I think that I was going to go to a painting class and sit with a bunch of old ladies and try to paint flowers I cringe. I'm so grateful that you put me on this path of discovery."

About six months later, we had a meeting, and I examined her mature and fascinating drawings. Yes indeed, she was ready to put them to canvas. I felt excitement at sharing her first choice to make a painting. We went carefully over the discovery elements of color and the similar investigations that would bring her color to the same level as her drawings. She played with the color for several months and still had not attempted to combine them with the drawing. It had been nearly two years since our shopping spree. She had devoted herself to the pursuit on a level I had never witnessed before, a complete emotional dedication that was on the fringe of obsessive. But, she was a special kind of person with a concentration level and ambition that we never discussed.

Because I had fears of her complete immersion into a state of complexities that I didn't understand, we had some conversations about breaks, and other means of escape from this wholly encompassing enterprise. I realize the depths involved as I disappear into a world of my own when painting and often cannot remember anything else during these long periods of concentration. We met again some months later, and she showed me that original drawing in color. She had done it many times over, but this was the result that she thought was her best effort. The picture was exciting and had most of the elements necessary for a good design. But the color, although mature and with good combinations and contrast, was not integrated into the drawing successfully. She knew this and was frustrated by the knowledge that it was not working. I told her that she had in less than three years covered more ground than anyone I had ever known in the past. We had a long and meaningful conversation about the integration of paint, line and graphic elements that play a part in this vision. She was impatient, and it was showing. I reminded her of the enthusiasm she had for the drawing and encouraged her to just play with the color and the line and give it another year of experimentation.

Over a period of the next several years, Barbara continued-- her dedication as strong as ever—and strived to put more elements into her work. She improved her design abilities, her construction instincts, and color. But, she did not have a natural feeling for the role that the color plays in the development of the drawing. There was a missing link which kept the work from being entirely satisfactory. Although, in reflecting on the work of that period, she was truly better than many of the artists that are considered important—in art—in the scheme of things. I instructed her to work very large; to see if working on a canvas four-by-six-feet would change her perspectives and elevate her into a better realm. It worked, and she did a very dynamic piece of work that was truly professional and accomplished. Barbara had arrived at this point after full dedication for seven years. Because she had begun to share her work and feeling with others, she gained significant admirers, sold paintings, but refused to enter the commercial environment of the galleries. She had financial independence so she could continue to grow and persevere with her desires.

Barbara is eighty years old now, still, paints every day, and even bought a new home with a large studio and storage for her many works. She has introduced realistic ghost-like images that seem to emerge from the shadows of her elaborate imagination in her most recent work. She seems content to just accumulate a body of work, not having any plans to exhibit. Her vitality and spirit are such that I know the decision she made to become an artist was perfect for her, as it has answered her ultimate question: Why are we here? The magic of her quest has provided it to her.

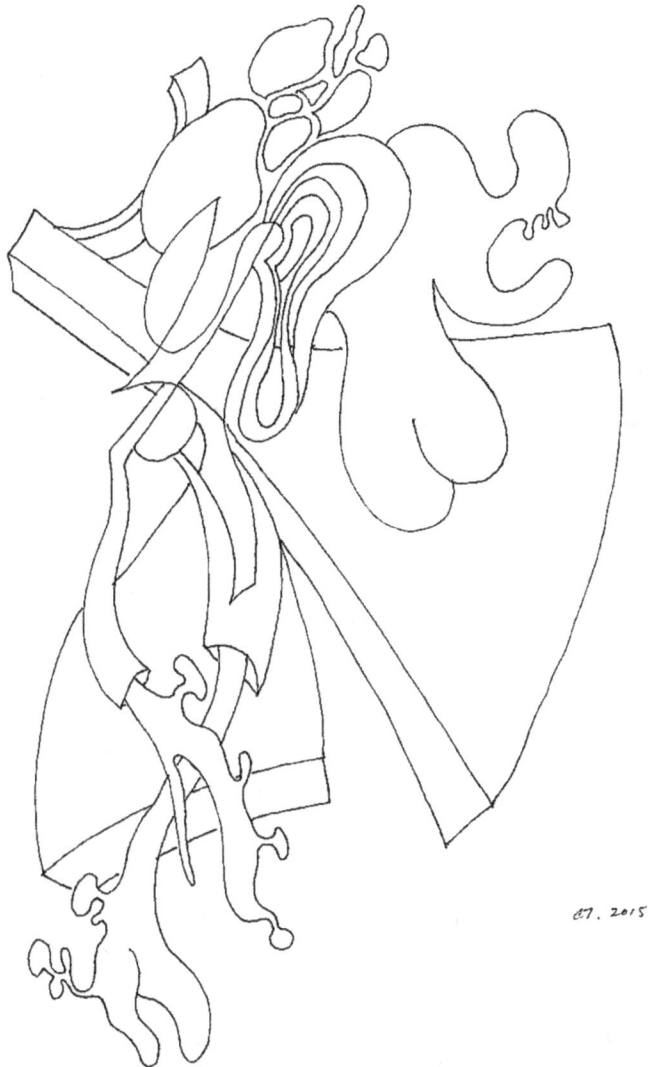

CHAPTER FOUR
Philosophies of Artists

I will not name the artist of this discussion as he is very well known. And although he has passed, I don't know that he would want me to divulge our conversations. So, for the sake of having a name, we will call him Tom.

I had returned to the United States from my studies in Europe and was making the rounds of the galleries and possible studio locations in Los Angeles. I went into a popular gallery on La Cienega Boulevard. The owner was a slightly plump, arrogant man in his late thirties. I approached him and told him my story and that I was looking for a gallery to represent me and also for a studio location. He looked down his nose at me and said, "We have more artists than we can handle." He dismissed me with a wave of his hand and went back to his desk. I looked at the divisional muddy canvases on his walls, and they did nothing for me. Just partitions of three or more spaces on a canvas with a combination of drab smoothly colored hard edge patterns. It was not a new experience. I had been treated with this kind of zero interest at a number of the more well-established galleries. They were successful in a field that was difficult, and I am sure that a hoard of artists approached them daily. But, as I recollected in Paris, when I would contact a gallery, they would say to please send them some color slides. Many galleries set up their projectors once each week, and reviewed artists work. If there were a further interest, they would visit the artist's studio.

In Los Angeles, over a significant number of years and the visiting of the galleries on a continual basis, I was never asked to visit my studio. If they had interest, they would ask me to bring some canvases to their gallery. I took this to mean that they were much more commercial in their thinking. It never occurred to them that the experience of seeing my—or any artists—studio might be exciting or fulfilling.

Some of the most incredible experiences of my life were the visiting a great talent's studio. When I think of this, one experience comes to mind. I was working with Rene Belzer in London, with her in the studio was the famous artist Oskar Kokoshchka, and we went to have lunch with an art dealer friend of hers. At the luncheon was another man. He was very quiet at first—his pristine appearance and demure posture gave me some clues to his character—but as the conversation turned to the evaluation of another artist's work, he became quite vocal and started to malign them with no reservations. He then contorted his smile and made light of his own criticism, and his nervous condition became evident. I asked him what he painted, and he said, "Brains and Heartbeats," then he smiled and said, "I would be happy to show you. Rene tells me you are a great artist."

The food was so terrible that I couldn't wait to get away from the smells that came from the kitchen. England at that time was heavily rationed, and the food was almost unbearable. After lunch, when we left the restaurant, he invited me to see his work. We proceeded to his studio in Soho. At first, the sight of his studio threw me into escape mode, I couldn't wait to get out of there. The rubble around me was in direct contrast to this well-presented man. I never suspected to see a studio like that, and I might add that never in my long career have I ever seen such squalor. This first impression along with the violent nature of his works was like someone had hit me on the head with a mallet. The work was demanding and disturbing but entirely fascinating.

He said nothing and just let me study and absorb what I was experiencing. We began to speak of the Paris atmosphere and my studies at the Beaux-Arts Académie, he asked a lot of questions, and we became deep in the comparison of what the young artists of Paris were doing. He did not attempt to ask or discuss his own work. I merely told him that it was dynamic and forceful. We were interrupted by his friend, and I was aware that he was gay and it might be a jealousy situation. We had lunch the next day and talked for a couple of hours, I brought a bold portrait that I had done of Rene to show him, and he said it was potent. There were future dealings with Francis Bacon, but that first encounter was indelible in my mind.

I don't think that seeing a few works brought to a gallery would give you even a hint of the real artist and his environment. The overall atmosphere of his studio and painting life is important and an essential entry into the overall understanding of his work, mentality, and personality. It is for this reason that very early in my career I insisted that a dealer come to my studio and understand my world and dreams. I told them bluntly that if they would not invest the time to really evaluate the work, I was not interested in their representation. I felt that after seeing several pieces of my work, reading my background and education, they would either be willing to invest the time or not. But, at least I would have the benefit of having full exposure.

Tom was a well- trained artist who had begun his career as a fabric designer. His early work was flimsy and shallow. He sold paintings to a group of middle-class working people who had little taste in art. During his struggle with working commissions in advertising and rug and fabric illustrations, he came under the influence of one of the major San Francisco Bay area figurative painters. The man was a knowledgeable philosophical giant. During this period, he made a transition that would bring him to an understanding and level to foster major recognition to his work.

He liked to do San Francisco scenes as he loved the city, but they were commercial renditions and ordinary subject matter. He began to look at the lines in the drawings and told me that they seemed to jump out at him; that they were the essence of the landscape. Then he decided that the city was a particular color scheme of closely related tones and values that could define and blend at the same time. He liked the idea that he could paint something that only he could see, a sort of monochromatic vision that emerged with examination. Then as he produced a volume of these works, he went back into them and clarified the structure and put bold highlights to exaggerate the drama. He told me that he had to re-evaluate his volumes and define his colors slowly as he developed the body of work as a whole. As his work became highly individual and recognizable, his audience grew, and his recognition skyrocketed. He had become immersed in visions and style, and the work took on new dimensions over the years. He had found the magic of his own mind and was able to synthesize his personal pleasures and visions until they became part of his inner being.

The images in nature, the challenge of capturing the human element, is the beginning of the quest. The understanding and ability to portray subjects is the first step in finding yourself and making a transition to executing a work of art with skill and clarity. But, traditional painting may be your desire and may fulfill the first passion for becoming an artist. It is unlikely that this endeavor would be a constant and fulfilling quest unless it is infused with elements of your personal images and colors. To merely be good at what has been done many times before is an empty shell that would not foster the passion and joy that could be attained with images which are generated from your own psyche. When one creates something that is genuinely personal, regardless of the maturity that is essential, the inner satisfaction is still there. Then it is only a matter of growth and consistent application of the emotional factor which guides your hand.

Every artist I have known that found their own avenue, slowly built upon it until it was individual and distinctive. Even at the point of great personal satisfaction and accomplishment the style and innovation continued to grow and become all-encompassing. The vital part that the artist must understand is that it is you and only you that you must please. The artist that paints for the accolades of others suffocates his own growth.

There is a distinction here. There are those that wish to occupy their time, play the role of the artist, and experiment with the reproductions of photographs, other art works and non-demanding aspirations that manifest in some simple and obvious images. The person who has no more ambition to perceive something beyond this state, should not consider themselves an artist. An artist assimilates art that has achieved significant recognition before them. Then takes that knowledge and infuses it with their personal reflections of all the images that have been encoded in their brain, those burned into his mind on their journey through life. This private sphere grows and materializes in the design, color and the magic of their creative powers. Consumed by experiments to portray their imagination, they will conquer the image and make it their own. Then they become an artist.

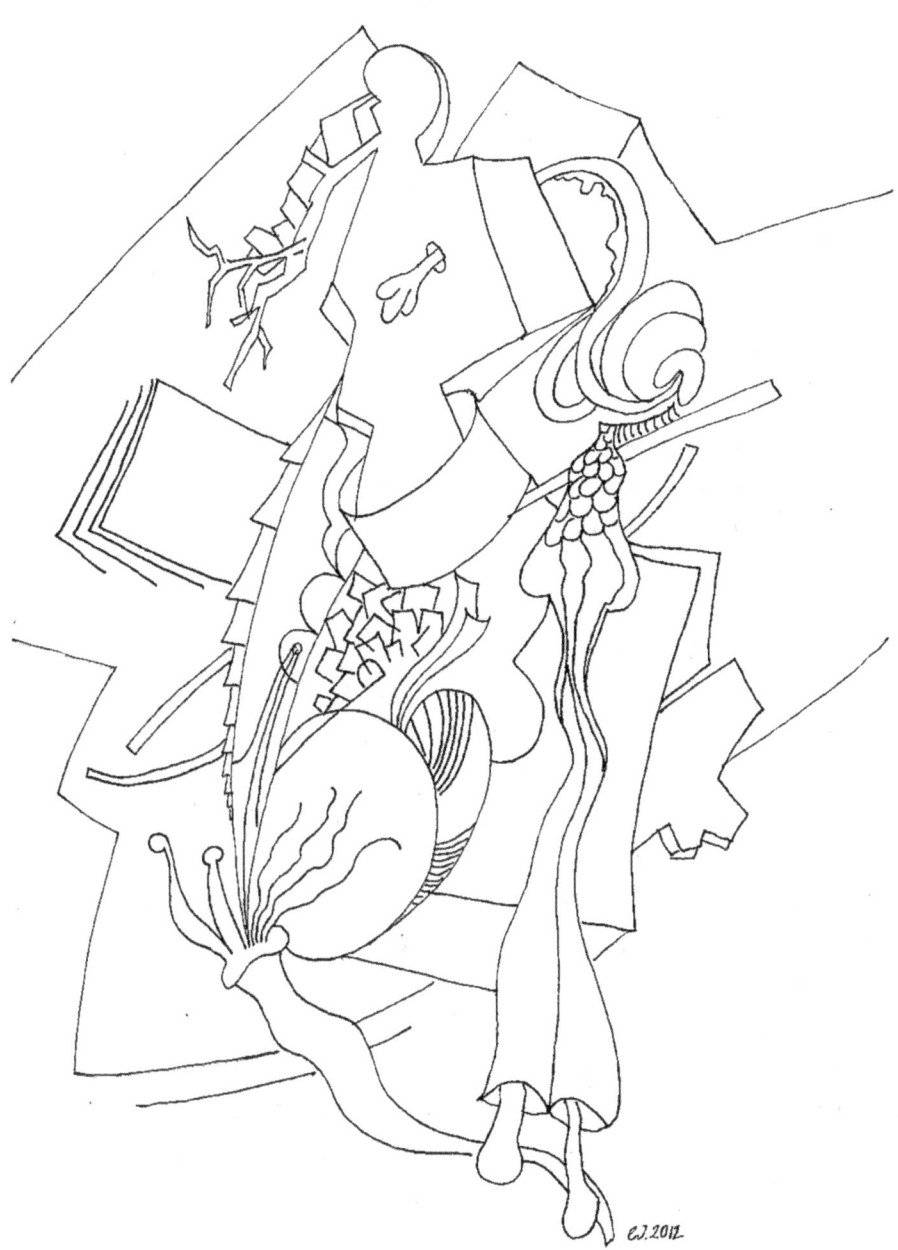

CHAPTER FIVE
The Magic

RECOGNIZING THE MAGIC OF SHAPES, VOLUMES, AND COLOR

We are constantly on a visual journey. Every view on our travels, every magazine, every photograph, every sight that we encounter has a pattern of its own, a particle of the elements that we see. Last night I was watching a television show of a musical presentation. The figures and shadows dancing with beams of spotlights, with the costumes and bright colors moving in patterns. I stopped the picture for some still images, then I ran it back to the beginning. I stopped in sequences to get to something that was almost an abstract, I progressed over and over again to find one image that brought the excitement and energy to my mind. When I found the magic moment, I sat and drew the image. I wrote notes about the colors I imagined would make it a personal statement. When I was finished, it was a design that I refined into a symbolic shape and color. When I examined it the next day I said to myself, this is a new addition to my alphabet of images and color. One finds these personal expressions during our expedition through life. They are the spark that lights your own fire.

There is a part of one's brain that absorbs and stores the sizes, shapes, and volumes of compelling images, not as a conscious recording but a subconscious reference that grows and becomes more available to the conscious mind when called upon. This is a matter of repetition and training, it takes years of refining, understanding and illustrating the personal imaginative symbols to make them work in a unified forum. Collect images, do not try to explain why you react and record them. Build a storage locker for your imagination without the verbal explanations to anyone, especially yourself. When the mind becomes so involved with the sights of your own creative recordings, a predominant cycle of images will emerge.

These recordings will start to enter into your drawings, and you will begin to synthesize the content and understand them as part of a whole concept. Remember that what you are pursuing is the infinite objective of your own world. Real personal art does not need to be shared. As a matter of personal feelings, I am at this point in my career not interested if others react or understand my work. When someone asks me to explain it, as often happens, I say to make of it what you wish. Much of it has some literal recognition, but the symbolism and personal language can only be evaluated with study and being exposed to many of my paintings and drawings.

When the vocabulary is sufficient to compose, one can draw a significant element of the desired subject and infuse it with the natural subjective relationship with the symbols that come to mind. As the language is used, the meanings become clearer to the artist and modifications to emphasize the intent grows, and often even becomes another symbol of his statement used to define more clearly his objective.

A natural distortion takes place when using this personal language, as the personality of the artist emerges on the canvas, when his imagination allows him to create his own world, and make all the adjustments to which color will contribute. Color is in itself a personal language, the sense of it must be treated the same as the design elements. They must become personal and exciting to the artist. If they are pursued diligently, it will all come together.

The critical issue with both the design and color is that the artist himself finds his joy and excitement with the discovery of elements within his own work. This continual finding of the magic portion leads to paintings that will be complete in their reflection of successful work. When you can stand back and feel that there are no additions or changes needed and that evaluation sustains over a period of time, then you have arrived at a level that stands out as a significant painting.

The pursuit of the above is not challenging, but it is a matter of personal freedoms. If even the slightest of invasion is present, then the purity of the quest is compromised. So, it is crucial that one is insulated from the influence and opinions of others, particularly artists. This guarded mental sphere is of particular importance in the first few years. Once one has established the work ethic and method of work, outside influences will be brushed off easily.

Finding that special place in the creative world is a worthy cause, once you possess it, it is yours, you own it. Then it is only the limitations imposed by our society, the presentation systems, the prejudice of the static and unimaginative world of androids that pass judgments on what they will never understand. When people look at the incredible photos of the Hubble telescope, they accept them and think they are beautiful. But when the artist creates his own world they look for some relationship to their limited exposure to images which are familiar. To accept and embrace something that is entirely new and perhaps distorted, or demanding, or unpleasant is rejected because of their refusal to grow. The uninformed and uninspired are the barrier to acceptance. There are two sides to this coin, the one you face and enjoy and the one that has no consequence.

WHEN IT FEELS RIGHT

Let's suppose that the new painter has copied a series of forms and shapes from various sources, such as underwater colored photographs, cactus shapes, and flowers, unusual plants, photos of sand dunes, rocks, and bacteria close-ups with the electron microscope and visions that excite him. He draws his mental portfolio a number of times. At some point, he will find what he has done is fun and exciting, and he knows that it feels right. He then draws the image on a canvas with a pencil so that he can alter various aspects and make a final statement. When he has created his vision, he then decides it is time to paint with his oil colors. Now he must find a palette that has the same elements as his drawing. He places strokes of paint on paper or board, with combinations of colors that please him. At some point, he will know what will be the right combinations to enhance his drawing. Then it is time to make the decisions of contrasts. He must weave his colors into the composition to improve the feeling of depth, and also the area's that he wants clearly defined and those which will remain soft and blend. Sometimes a line must be fixed, stark and bold, at other times it is fluid like a stream. It is the variety of line, color, shapes almost lost and those amorphous areas enhanced by the softness and strength of color that make the overall concept emerge. Keeping these issues in mind and satisfying one's inner feelings will find its place, and you will know it is right.

Each time you paint a picture, the images will mature; the design elements will become more sophisticated, and the color will become a part of your understanding. Finding a particular area in your own work will foster new ideas that will slowly grow into an individual style. Identification is a key to gaining an audience, as your work progresses. The elements that identify you will come naturally, providing you do not succumb to the opinions of others. You will gain a natural tendency to size, you will know when the drawing is meant to be large or small. The repetition will be a body of work that expresses you and only you. After several dozen canvases, you will have found the elements in each area that are your own. When the style is mature, and you have reached a consistency, it is time to utilize this same method in other approaches, introduce various elements, figures, shadows, landscape and the imagination and fantasies that emerge from the canvas itself.

The feeling of standing back and being absorbed by the creation you have produced, knowing it is entirely original and of your own mind and imagination, is one of singular magic in a world of imitations and pretense.

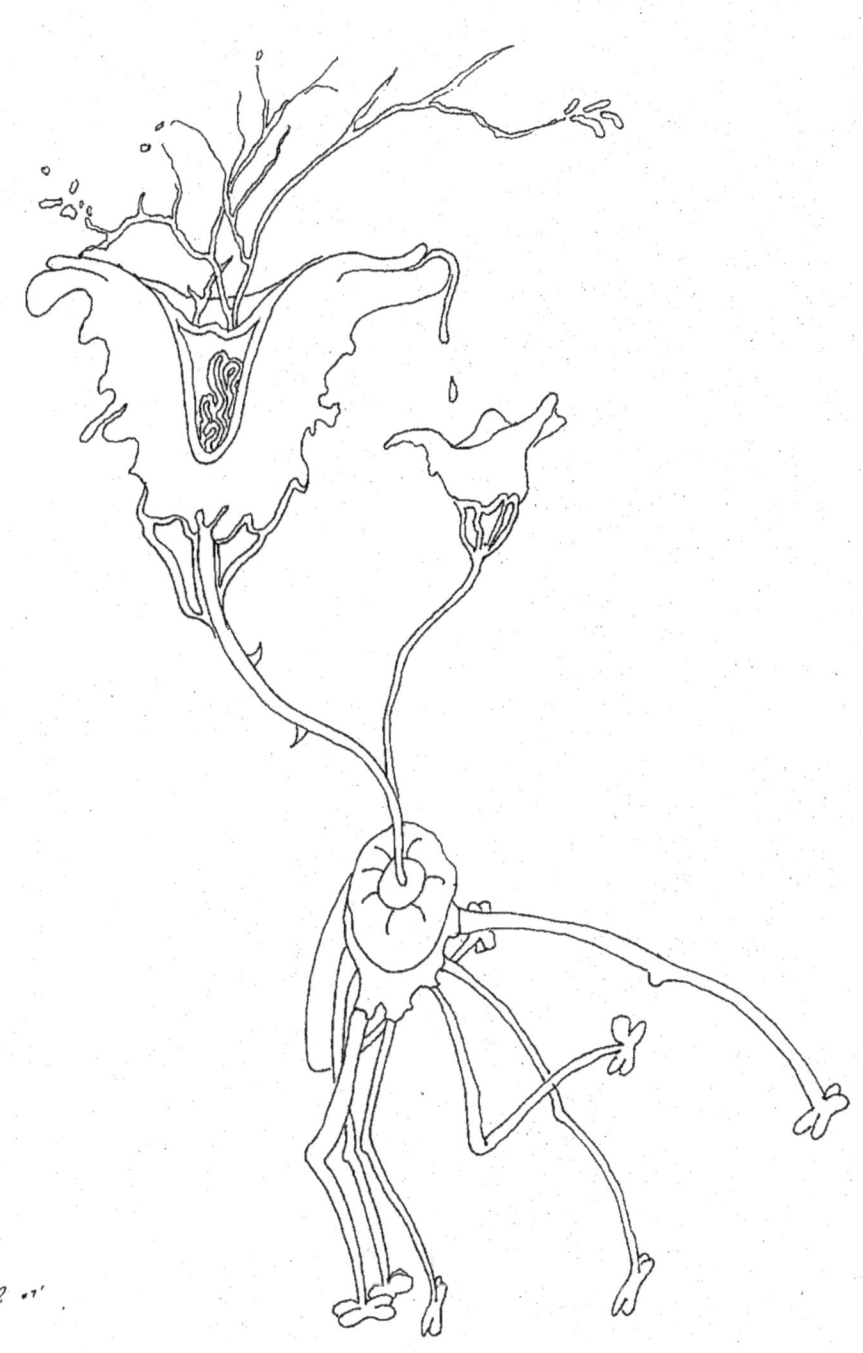

CHAPTER SIX
Understanding the Reasons

Talent, recognized by collectors of the artist presented, attracts prospective buyers. Artists being aware of the importance of these avenues of promotion, seek to make their work appeal on that basis. The majority I have known look to find what is popular, what is selling, sometimes in a general sense but often directly copying the style and subject matter. This bandwagon approach is evident when a local artist has a very successful show and receives the press, the purchases and the recognition that nearly every artist is seeking. There are many, however, that adhere to their personal philosophies and pursue in-depth investigations into the specific areas of their interests. It is only when such an artist is brought to the forefront of recognition—and financial success—that others start to pursue the same objectives. But, nearly all of those secondary—derivative—artist's pursuits are understood on a surface level, rarely producing original and meaningful works.

THE FUN AND FULFILLMENT ELEMENT

The word fun is often discarded as a shallow view of art, just as the word decorative has a connotation of something less than serious. But, just because it is fun to execute or to view does not mean that it is not also emotionally rewarding, profound and meaningful. A clear and defined personal statement can be fun as well. It is not a dirty word! I do not discard the word serious, and yes, I do like and enjoy work by those who are morbid and produce profound and disturbing images that haunt the soul. It is all part of the creative process. My preference is HAPPY but infused with all the elements of the above. The imagery can be a sleight of hand entry into all facets of the imagination. The brighter avenues and dark alleys housing a variety of angels and monsters living in dreams and dungeons, the more the complexities intrigue the mind of the artist. What it is... is fun! Because it is the magic of the mind and the joy of recording.

Whether the presentation is hanging on a wall in a museum or an individual's home, the first impression is the overall impact of the color and design. If the design has energy, space, and flow, it captures the eye immediately. If it also has lovely coordinated color that emotionally involves the viewer, this decorative aspect adds to the initial impact. This appeal does not alter the fact that if upon closer evaluation it is intricate, meaningful and emotionally charged. Other shapes, symbols and graphic statements within the design can harbor richer, complex assessment with colors that invade the inner realm of the work.

THE ART HOAX

We live in a world of advertising and promotion, the brainwashing vehicle to beat the potential purchaser into a state of numb reactions guided by manipulated mechanisms. The same is also true in the art world. Artists are bringing in millions of dollars that inherently do not have the design, color or imagination to qualify for any interpretation of talent or greatness. The unaware brainwashed by the uninformed, who join the great bandwagon of admirers that elevate artists for all the wrong reasons.

THE ART INVESTMENT

Art is a terrible investment, despite that, you can point out many individual cases where its value has grown faster than almost any other you can identify. But, overall it will never produce the returns of good solid investment practice. Speculation is not the reason to buy art, it is the first reason not to buy art! If you are encouraged to purchase an artist based on the fact that their prices are increasing, that would be a warning sign that you are being advised by the wrong person.

Many artists became very popular and their work advanced into some impressive numbers, but ten or twenty years later those same works when put at auction have brought only a small fraction of their cost at the height of their popularity. Although there is a value factor, some artists make such simplistic renditions that the level of time and effort involved is very minor. Then there are the artists that invent very involved designs and studied approaches and must spend endless hours to produce something of such complexities. Your judgment and study will give you a good read on this understanding; you must factor in the age of the artist, their background and exhibiting history.

In the end, you will know what is reasonable to buy or to price your own work. It is an individual judgment call, and only you in your understanding of your personal capacities and resources can make it. The auction houses play a significant role in the values set for the various better-known artists. But, often purchases can be made well below the gallery price. This is a dangerous path, as many of the works are a name only and the work itself does not have the value that the unsuspecting collector imagines. It is always prudent to have the advice of a professional art dealer that you trust to guide you in this kind of purchase. I have known many that have bought at auction with the full blessing of the curators of the firm, only to have some expert many years later disqualified the work as a copy.

THE NUMBER ONE REASON TO BUY

Why should we paint? Why should we buy?

To add a window; the painting becomes one! I'll explain. Let me propose that you own a home or live in an apartment. Some windows provide a view that gives dimension to that living space. You could not imagine not being able to look out at something. The more interesting the view, the more pleasure it gives you. But there are blank walls. They confine you in that space, stifle your freedom. If we add a large painting beautifully done, it gives you another window. A landscape will open up a view to something or someplace that inspires you or provides you with a remembrance of something special. Perhaps you love flowers and patterns, it can give you a window to that love of the things you cherish.

But, even the window to the best view possible will become static in time, and the impact will dissipate. So, if we are to create a new window, it is important that the talent of the artist be such that his rendition is beyond just a static photographic image. He must infuse it with a magical potion of interest and charm to bring it alive. But, there are several steps beyond this choice. You can have a window into the mind, the imagination and magic of another brain, a journey never quite completed because the road is challenging and demanding. This can be a bright spot or many bright spots in your home to energize and create windows of the mind.

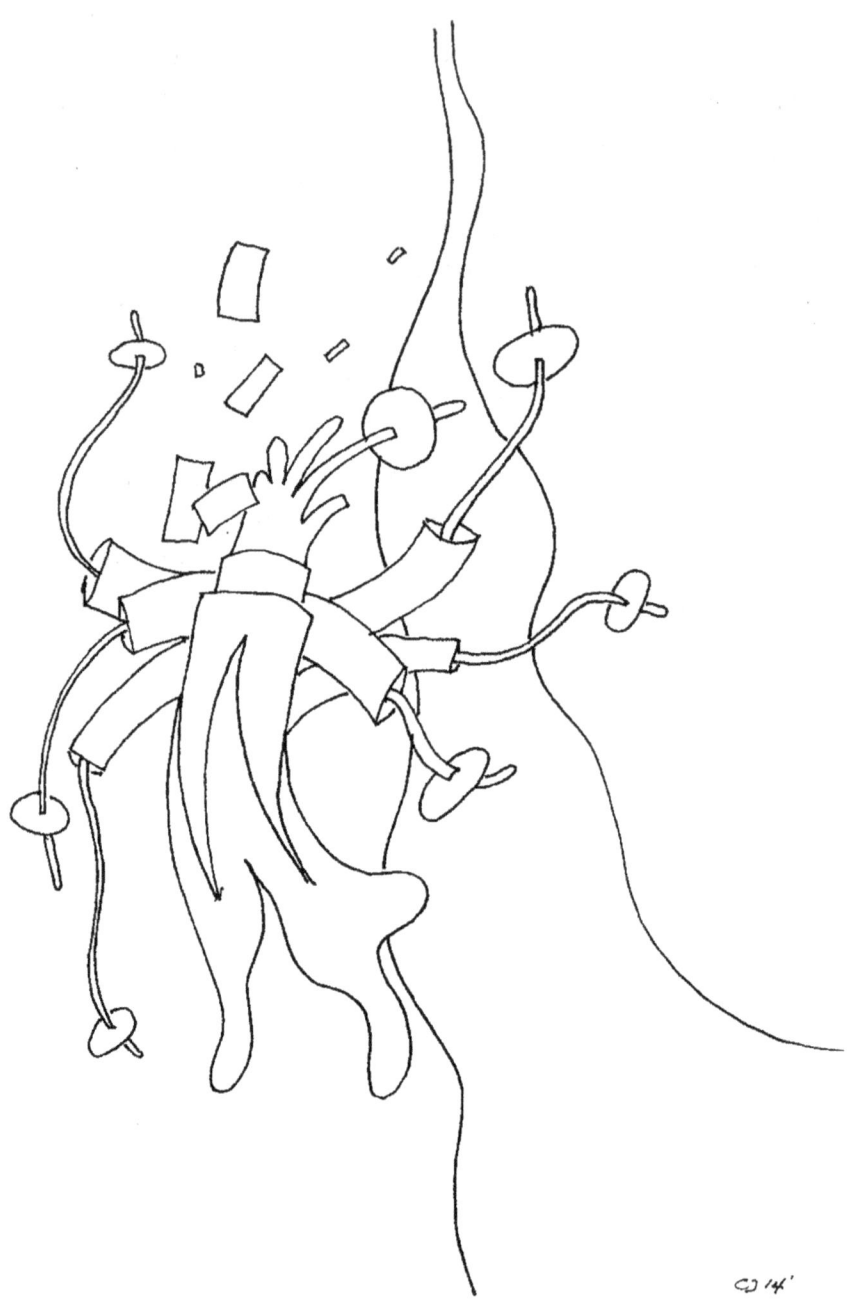

CHAPTER SEVEN
Imagination & Creativity

Imagination comes first, then the creative drive uses this information and finds a path to utilize all the elements of that thought. To think outside of the box, as they say, is essential to decipher the point imagined. There are many ways to say something in a different language that may be foreign to the viewer. Invent the images that become your personal symbols to express your passion and understanding. Follow your path and continue to work on each new canvas with similar images and fresh, original images. Each time setting it aside, yet maintaining the momentum. When you finish with your images clearly stated, and the canvas is believed complete. Then it is time to wait and evaluate at some point in the future. There will be a strong desire to go back and critique the beginning. Then in succession, you will find that the re-evaluation and the adding of elements to improve and clarify your thoughts, will manifest in making the work more definable in your mind. You will start to know what you have done is a complete statement. It does not matter if at this stage it has become so individual, so unique to your vision and conception, that others do not comprehend. If you feel in your heart that you have contributed a particular note in the scale that is the foundation that will build the career of contentment and joy.

Having exposure to all forms of images is essential. The drawing of them imprints it on your brain. Let's say that each day you draw something entirely foreign to you: machine gears, motor parts, umbrellas, weird plants of the tropics—things you've never paid attention to in the past nor had any dealings with. Each time you absorb these and refine them to the essentials, you are increasing your vocabulary. Next, take the drawings and combine images: a tropical flower with machine gear parts, or underwater soft coral colors and pictures. Each investigation into the imagery and designs that surround us will motivate you to invent more interesting paintings. Often, I utilize images conceived in one of my drawings and integrate it into the fabric of a semi-realistic landscape or figure. This is something that amuses me and brings me flights of fanciful thoughts that manifest in many pleasures.

When the work reflects a new world of shapes, designs and personal images, familiar forms will emerge. When you examine a cloud formation, a pattern in the earth or rocks, often you see faces and details that bring forth imagined landscapes and figures and familiar scenes. You can build upon these images and infuse the painting with more tools for the viewer to capture the illusory.

The growth of your abilities to synthesize the designs and the maturity of applying color with the coordination and understanding of the texture and brush stroke will lead you to integrate some realistic images. This path will be refined into an expansion of your knowledge and abilities to infuse the work with more ideas, thus leading you to become a better technician. It is a reversal of the traditional approach to learning to draw and paint. Instead of the frustration and discouragement found in fighting your way through an ABC beginning, you are starting with the more exciting and more stimulating aspects of art, and thus your approach is easier and more fun. Remember, the essence of art is not the ability to reproduce like a camera, it is the power of your imagination and creativity.

I cannot emphasize enough the importance of letting it flow and making it enjoyable. Your first painting could be a messy and terrible looking effort. But, it is your private world, and it is not to be shared. Use canvas boards for your first attempts. When you have a half-dozen or so of your work, sit down put them in a row and spend an hour or so evaluating what areas you like and what is not interesting. By synthesizing your work, you will discover unique parts you can build upon. As your imagery grows and expands through the drawing and investigations with ink and paper, it will be translated with greater ease each day that you work. Color should also be part of the study and evaluation of the work by others, of fabrics, and photographs. With this avenue of your art adventure, think of yourself as an untamed purveyor of change, a rebel in the world of images.

There are fun and pleasure in painting that escapes many artists that become overwhelmed by the absence of understanding and lack of interest from others. Those circumstances weigh heavily on them. First, you must appreciate that the further you venture into this private world the more people you leave behind. In time, there will be only a handful of people who have any idea of what you are pursuing. Is it vital that you have this audience? No, it is not. When the work is mature and accomplished, a small but significant audience will find you. Then the importance of promotion and strategy takes place. Do you think that when Albert Einstein was creating the equations on the massive number of pages to define the Theory of Relativity, he had people around him that understood and appreciated his quest? I think not! In a way, it is the path itself that is the accomplishment. The strength of conviction that comes with knowing you have added something of value to the world. I am in agreement with those who feel that they wish just to create something that is beautiful and acceptable to society. There are those who consider this the pinnacle, and I understand it is a necessary part of the equation. But, it can never spawn the elation of pure thought and creativity of those who venture beyond the limits of wonder.

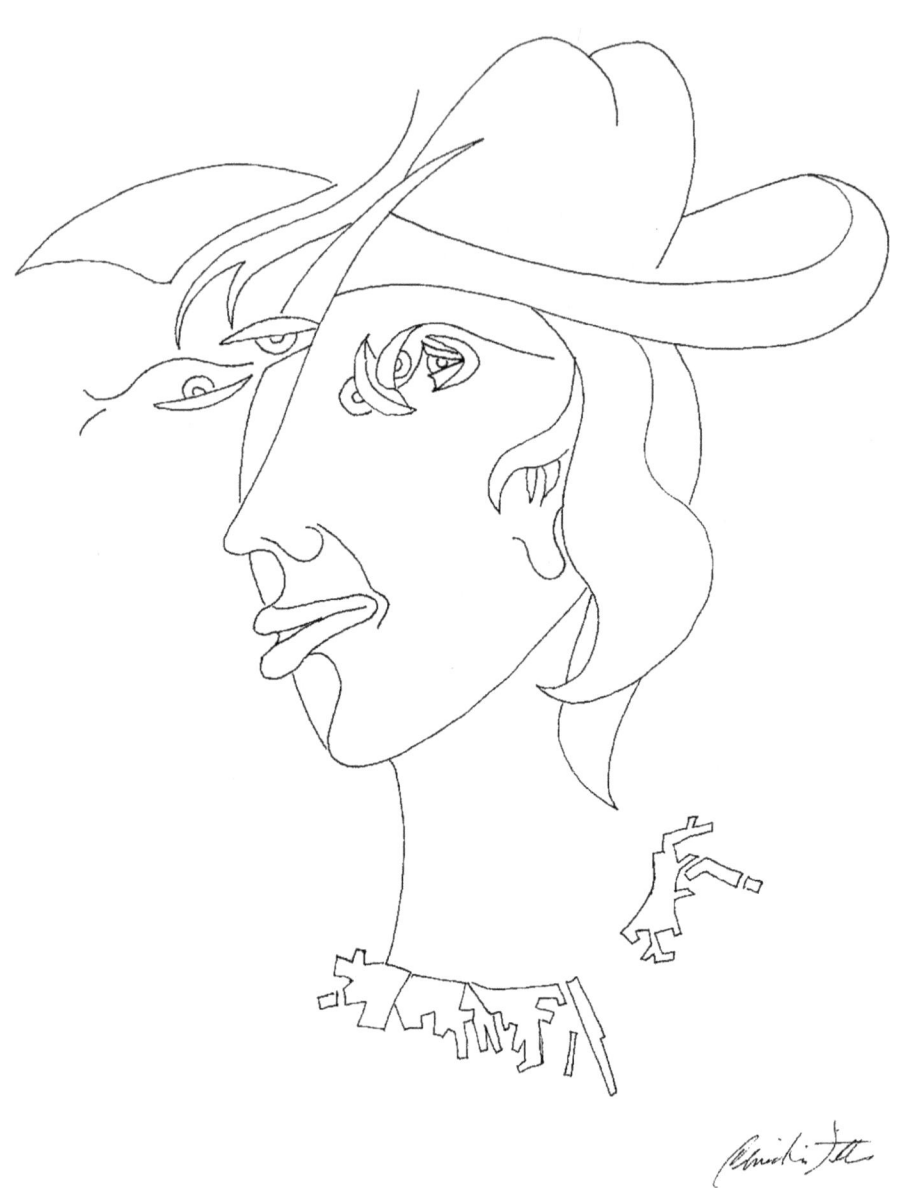

CHAPTER EIGHT
Paint for Yourself

I have heard it said many times, that there is no escape. That you are a prisoner of your background and the accumulated history that defines your path in life. That you cannot escape from yourself. I disagree, but first... what is escape? One form is physical, but a far more interesting is mental: leaving the present but going nowhere but places within our mind. When we drive our car to a familiar destination, we arrive, and the realization hits us that we do not remember part or nearly all of the journey. What happened? The boredom of the tedious and the lack of a need for conscious thought caused us to escape momentarily. We can flee for seconds, hours and even permanently. When we slip away from all the realities, we enter into a mental state sometimes labeled with unpleasant names. Can we control then this venture into the land of imagination and fantasy? Yes, we can. It is the avenue for the mind to create exciting voyages into unknown worlds. There are many in literature, music and the art world that have pioneered successfully into the magic land of creativity. The arts are many means of escape where one can venture into other realms of experience, glamour, fantasy, and dreams. It is important to realize it is not merely an escape, but a healthy pursuit and relief from the pressures, demands, and absurdities of modern society.

It is for this reason that it is a solo journey not to be shared until the artist can control their artistic efforts, so they remain unaffected by the actions and opinions of others. When they can enter into that state of mind at will and can perform their craft with the tools developed, they are strong and independent enough to withstand the onslaught of the ignorant.

The artist's tools—I mentioned above--of imagination are found through investigation into every imaginable shape and color in our universe. A particle theory that encompasses from the minute to the finite. One must think in broad terms and absorb the philosophies of the absolute to the absurd. It is when one begins to reproduce the shapes, designs of all the modern exposures and infuse them with the colors of new and strange worlds of nature and science that emerges and becomes a new reality. We have pictures taken by the electron microscope of bacteria, insects, human parts and photographs from the Hubble telescope, close up photographs of rock formations, sand, plants, and human components. It goes on and on, there is no limit to the wonderful world of shapes and forms and colors.

In the beginning, there is pen and paper. I prescribe pen because if you make a mistake, or you are not happy with what you have drawn, you must not erase. It is the comparison of the results that give insight into what the final rendition should be or that it becomes. It is a game of sketching those images that fascinate the mind and lead to a continuous path to that other dimension. That is what becomes the FUN factor, and keeps you pursuing and enjoying the craft.

When you have developed your favorite shapes and designs, and the drawing looks back at you and says it is time, the color invasion begins. Investigate the colors with the same drive that you found in the images you recorded. Play with the color and feel the joy of that added gift. Repeat the color renditions the same as you did the drawings. You will find in art history where many great artists painted the same picture over and over again with a variety of colors. To paint in series is an exciting pursuit and very rewarding. Even if you feel that an effort is not successful, keep it and study, analyze it at future times. There will be evaluations later that add to your abilities, there will even be complete reversals of your opinions. In the final examination, this escape can be a rewarding and stabilizing factor that strengthens your core being and supports a foundation for understanding and confidence.

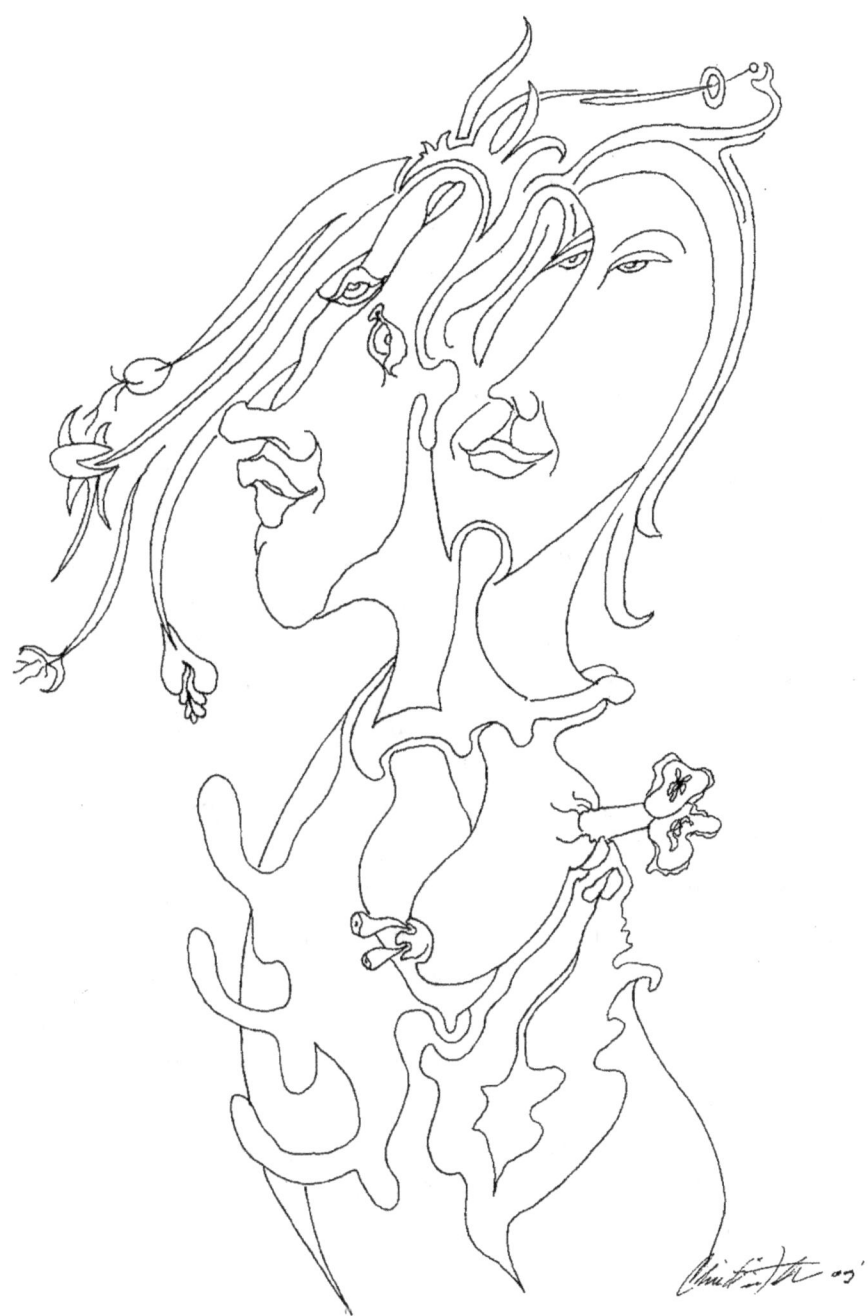

CHAPTER NINE
The Studio

Having a studio with a good north light is essential and having the materials at hand and the tools of your trade is part of the stage setting. When you paint, you do not want to have any concerns about anything that might be missing. You must be isolated without phones ringing or interruptions that break your train of thought. You must get lost in the execution of your images and color. When immersed entirely in your painting, a subjective emotional force will guide you to new discoveries.

Paint many canvases and collect a body of work where you can review and contemplate the improvements that would enhance the painting. Repeat the images that inspire you, changing the color, design and finish to adhere to your new-found sensibilities. When you have completed a painting that you feel has reached the level of your desires and goals, transpose it to a large canvas. Build upon that success. This will give you new dimensions and foster inventive aspects of the work. In time, all of these elements of drawing, color, and execution will become instinctive, and the resulting work will be a testament to your dedication and inspiration. Do not be discouraged by the lack of interest and understanding from friends and family. The average person has no desire to even spend any time looking and feeling something about a work of art. You are entering a limited and exclusive world and the further you delve into your painting the more isolated you will become. This is the bonus of your quest, you will find the few that will become your partners of understanding, and they will be more important than all of the masses of humanity that pass your way.

In these pages, I have purposely avoided the discussion of sculpture, collage, and mediums other than the use of oil paints. Acrylics have their place, but I have no use for them as they do not have the plasticity and feel of oils, and the life expectancy is very limited, the pigments are weak, and the tinting power is not strong. So, I will stick with the premise that oil is the most satisfying and presents the most flexibility in the application. The drawback is of course that the fumes are damaging to the health, so the use of exhaust fans and good circulation is an absolute necessity. There are odorless paint thinners, and I use them, but one must be especially cautious with their use as they are as damaging as those with the heavy odor.

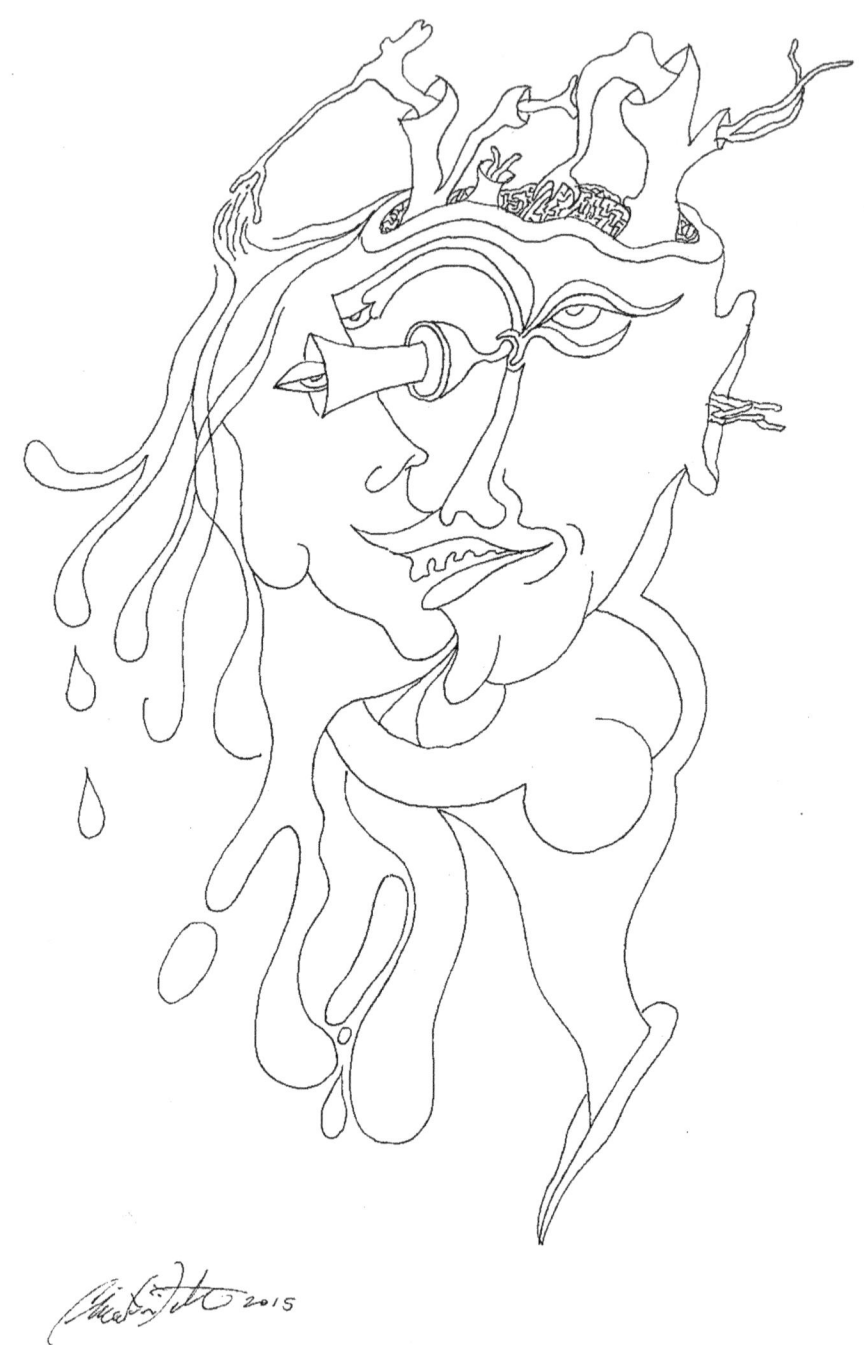

CHAPTER TEN
Identifying Style

THE IMAGES MANIFEST INTO A SPECIFIC STYLE

A drawing style will emerge with the continuing investigation of shapes and forms, volumes and details. Familiar images will bring new challenges in the quest for finding what is satisfying within. Many shapes and designs will be repeated as the artist considers those which have particular appeal. As they develop, realistic images will emerge from their machinations. Because certain developments will take place with the repetition, they will adopt these and make them part of their personal vocabulary. As one finds the hidden images in nature, they will provide the revelation of secrets of individual expressions. Always be aware that the accidental is often the road to the most captivating elements of the work.

During the 1940s and 50s, the Abstract Expressionists developed dynamic personal expressions that brought emphasis for the first time in the Western world. It was the most powerful movement in American Art. Many of the proponents of this group used robust active and even violent actions to apply the paint. And there is a considerable validity to the spontaneous application. It reflects energy, boldness, and the integration of color on a scale that is captivating. On the other side of the coin, there are the hard edge formalists that make multiple complex divisions with colors that hold a particular fascination because they are the parts of a bigger picture of understanding. Using and experimenting with these ideas are the stepping stones that will lead you to your magic formula of progress.

Although I believe it is essential for the beginning artist to isolate himself for the first few years and to limit his exposure to photographic recordings of the shapes and forms in nature and space. It is also important to study the psychological aspects of imagination and creativity. The expansion of ideas and traditional avenues of creative thought will inspire the artist to greater fantasies in recording the shapes and forms. The forms can take place in pure thought; they can have unique shapes, complicated structures and magical and inspiring colors. This concentration can be repeated and conserved and recorded. When you learn to control imagery in your mind, by evaluating, changing and developing it, you will become ever closer to having the ability to register these images on paper or on canvas. Once recorded, the process of adding, subtracting, simplifying or complicating the vision becomes easier.

I had an artist friend who was a handsome and fascinating man. He had been well-trained and was very proficient at commercial illustrations. His work was in demand by the advertising agencies, and he made a comfortable living for his family. He did small intimate figurative oils which were very popular in his local gallery. I remember the opening evening of his exhibit when the entire show sold. I was excited for him and a little set back because of his lack of enthusiasm. Several weeks later, I called him to have lunch. He asked if he could come to my studio and we would eat somewhere nearby. At my studio, he scrutinized my work and was very complimentary about the direction I was pursuing. This happened in a period after a trip where I had rented a house in Guaymas, Mexico. The light there was so intense that I had investigated Fauvism on a level that had not been previously attempted. The bold, pure color was pronounced with a black outline, arbitrary to the recording aspects of the light. I was working continually toward a light so intense that it was entering the realm at risk of being washed out as if you had looked into the sun and your color intensity was then limited by the recovery of the retina.

At lunch, my friend explained that he had been doing his illustrations for twenty-five years and showing his small oils for more than fifteen years. His last three shows had sold out on opening night, and the gallery was always asking for more work. I asked him,

"Why don't you just paint the small oils and abandon the commercial illustrating?"

He replied, "I like dealing with the agencies and the art directors. They present me with stimulating challenges. I don't care much about the finished product, but it is a different objective each time that keeps me interested. I'm bored with the small oils, too. When I see you working with large canvases and progressing into new ideas and developing these works with outrageous color and force, I feel like a timid little midget in a cage. I need to break out into something, but I don't know where to go."

I said, "Keep your eyes and ears open, and somehow, somewhere in the next few weeks or months you will experience something that knocks you out with the beauty, horror, contrast or whatever. When this sight or experience is strong, concentrate on it, study it, make it your own and follow that path as far as your imagination will take you. That will open new doors, and you will find something special in the pursuit."

Six months later he called and asked me to come to his studio. He had always worked out of his home, and when he said to visit his studio, it was a surprise. When I arrived, I heard the new story. He was spending three days each week on the small figurative works that were paying the bills. With a wife and two children, one in high school and one in university, he had to keep some of his previous life going. His wife had returned to teaching school, so the pressure was not too great. He said he had been sitting in his backyard on a sunny afternoon when he started watching the shadows of his tree, trellis, and arbor on the white wall of his neighbor's garage. There was a spectrum of color reflecting from various angles which infused the white and shadow with slight accents just here and there. He drew the shadow in pencil, exaggerating some of the interesting designs that appeared before him. He thought it could be an exciting exhibit with the shadows on varying degrees of background colors and highlights from reflecting sources. He took his camera out that afternoon and then on through the next month he spent a considerable amount of time searching for and recording shadows. The array of images he had drawn on his studio walls was spectacular. He had already done about ten canvases of considerable size. Odd illustrations of wild shadow formations with outlines and bright, hard edge lines that were transparent and solid taking the viewer in and out of a spectrum of levels. I was impressed and could see the appeal and the fascination of his images immediately. It was further proof that the artist, if true to his own inner understanding and desires, could find a personal approach that inspired, excited and could still be successful.

His art dealer was not happy. He had built a following with his clientele for the small oils, and the new work was beyond his understanding. But because of commitment to the artist, he showed it and surprisingly found that he had some conversions and a whole new audience. The new work was now in the sphere of many New York galleries, and his agent for the commercial work contacted a friend, and a show was scheduled in that city. It was powerfully accepted and launched a much more exciting and lucrative career.

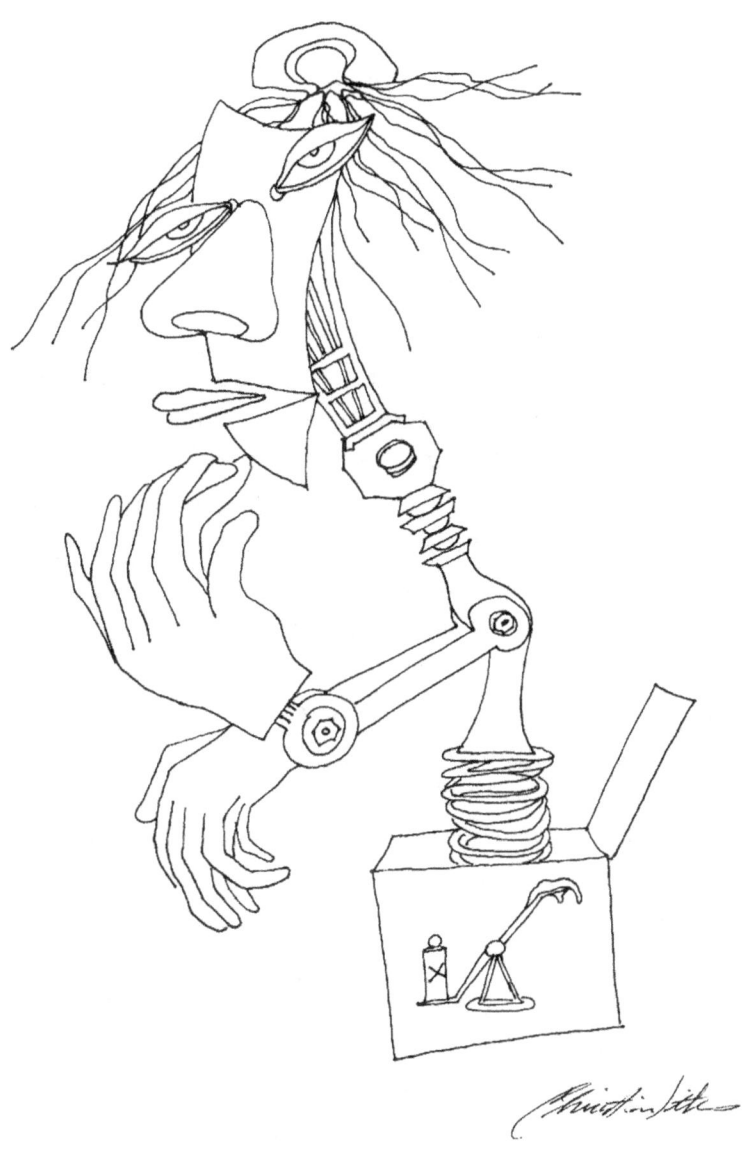

CHAPTER ELEVEN
Techniques

COLOR GAMES

There are some fun experiments with color that you can play with to get a feel for the elasticity of the paint and the utilization of the textures that come with using various mediums. In general, a paint thinner or turpentine is used to thin the paint and get the right creamy texture to make it flow as you wish. It is also generally used to clean your brushes. I use an industrial soap called Lava Soap to make the final cleansing of my brushes and to soften the bristles. I use Ivory Soap to clean my sable brushes as the harsher grain of the industrial soap damages the fine hairs. The reason for the additional cleansing is to keep the brushes pliable for the next use.

When using a solvent, the paint dries within a day to the point that it cannot integrate with the new application of paint. Although it is still wet to the touch, if you wish to work in a wet and juicy manner it will not be as satisfactory as using an oil medium. The paint will remain in a workable damp state for two to three days when using a linseed or walnut oil. The drawback to using an oil medium is that the finished work will take several weeks to have an entirely dry surface. With combinations of a thinner and an oil medium, a drying time can be adjusted to match your methods.

By experimentation, you should paint both dry and wet to see the various effects that are possible with each technique and different combinations. I use both depending on the effects to best capture the images I wish to portray. Usually, a painting will be consistent in the overall finish so only one method would be used on that particular work of art. This is a matter of choice as many artists use both techniques on a single painting. In the historical sense, combinations of oil and turpentine were applied in various degrees depending on the schedule and effects desired by the artist. Oil and oil paints were used in an opaque manner and also used with transparency for glazing and to achieve a surface depth and glow. These techniques of the past are seldom used today, but there are multiple choices for the artist, who with sufficient time will experiment with many variations of mediums.

Playing with color swatches and placing them in positions to expose only a small area or a large area will aid you as you explore the possibilities. In a class I was teaching, I had the students make four-inch square color boards. Some had as many as thirty or more to play with. I had them use a rectangular 12 x 16- inch black mat to frame the colors and sometimes they played with them for hours to get something that they felt was right. By description or numbers, they recorded the palette they wished to use. The volumes were dictated by the final choices of the framed colors. We evaluated them in the class, and each individual was entirely different in his decisions because it was mainly an emotional response and a purely personal one. It was satisfying and reinforced their confidence in the palette they were to use. I could see that it was a fun experiment each time I did this, and they gained a new understanding.

Once the choice of the drawing and color is made, and the decision of working wet or dry is decided, the execution then is simplified. I have had students that made interesting and acceptable efforts from the very beginning. In many cases, they have duplicated the same work several times, knowing they could improve with each canvas. The individual will naturally come to the combinations that please him most. But, just like with concentration on the drawings and paintings, they must isolate their experiments, not sharing them with others so that the conclusions are unbiased. Over a period of time, the character of their color will identify their personal touch and like the drawings will become consistent in their choices. They must decide what is subtle and what they will use to supercharge particular works with emotional and dramatic line and color. The impact of these decisions will develop with time and repetition.

In time, the artist will find within these works an emerging image, strange, comical, weird, haunting, ghost-like or mysterious. These findings are the key to the personal realm of your creativity. Then it is time to develop these happenings into your vocabulary. Do not be bound by tradition or mimic what others have done. It only matters if it is meaningful to you, and only you. Artists that have pursued this approach have found few viewers that will respond. But the sophisticated and imaginative that is moved by this undercurrent of imagination become dedicated on a level that is beyond that of casual friends and the general audience.

I remember a particular canvas that I painted on the banks of the Seine, in Paris during my student years. I sent it home to my mother as I was quite proud of the results. She loved it. I did not see that painting for some years and had forgotten about it. When I saw it again and was disappointed in what I saw, I said nothing. When my mother died nearly twenty years later, I got the painting back. I examined it in my studio for several weeks trying to recapture the feeling when I had painted it and to justify the technique and color. After considerable evaluation, I decided to paint a new rendition of the work with my current style and color sense. While pursuing that I started to understand better the influences and reasons for my previous approach. My second rendition was not really satisfactory. I did a third painting and infused it with a combination of the two styles. It was moderately successful, and I liked it better than the first two works. But, it was not ultimately satisfactory. I left the three works in the corner of my studio for several months, taking them out for assessment on several occasions. Finally, about a year later I decided that I had figured out the problem. I did a fourth painting and felt it was very successful. I remember this as a great learning experience. There was an improvement in all of my impressionist works after that experiment.

When you repeat a painting with new inspiration, there is a critical learning curve even if you exaggerate and distort and change the whole mode of approach. I have in the past taken an impressionist work and made it highly expressionistic and almost abstract. In other cases, I have seen imagery in the abstract forms and developed it into a lyrical practically literal subject. I believe that a painting can call you to it with an emotional attraction to foster another approach.

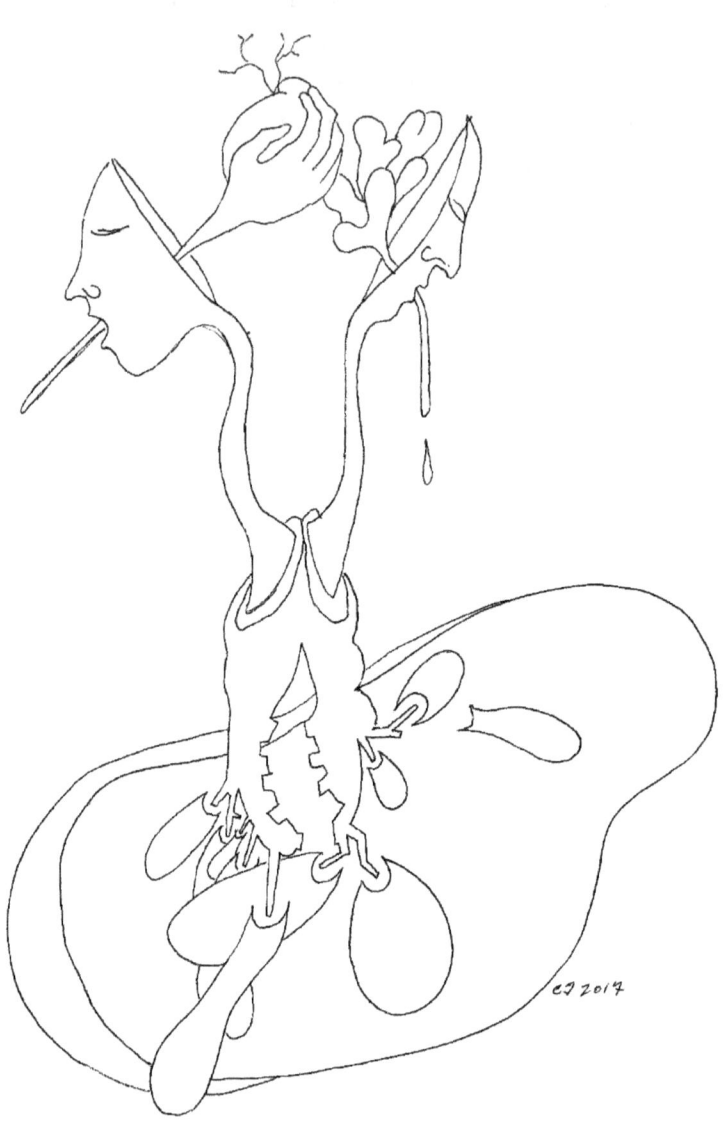

CHAPTER TWELVE
The Reference Library

The individual drawings recorded in your collection of sketchbooks are the foundation of your reference library. As an example, you have sketched the intricate design of a succulent from a photographic display of plants. The design differs from the photograph, and you have executed it several times, changing the form and developing it in a direction that in the final interpretation is something you feel is interesting and distinctive. Take this drawing from your sketchbook and insert it in your reference book or file. The series of these drawings from many sources, developed individually to the point that you find the excitement and confidence sustains, is the reference for the combining of images to render them to the stage that they become the material for your paintings.

These sketch notes in your file collectively are the material for the personal language—the alphabet and vocabulary—that will identify you in your work. Drawing and the execution will become second nature and pen in hand becomes part of your being. The creative energy will grow, and drawing will become a joy and source of great satisfaction. The work will continually take on new dimensions, and it will foster designs, with elements purely of your own psyche. Ultimately you will develop patterns and a style uniquely your own. Repetition breeds a level of confidence and the use of your creative powers that will manifest in images which subconsciously deliver an accomplished manner. This language will become so familiar it will reveal in your paintings without even a conscious application.

When a finished drawing has combined a number of the elements from this library, and you feel that the volumes, space, and design are a cohesive success, it is time to translate to canvas. After the drawing is completed and ready for color, you refer back to your library of color. All of the color experiments which have resulted in combinations that have had an emotional impact and now have taken their place in your reference library, are examined and chosen because you feel it has an affinity to the drawing on the canvas. This is the stage that is the most exciting. You must now decide if you wish the image to be amorphous, hard edge or a combination of hard and soft lines. Will this be executed with an oil medium to keep it wet and juicy, fluid and spontaneous, or will it be dry, blended, shaded with nuances of contrasts? This becomes another experimental facet of your quest. You may try one and then the other or a multitude of combinations. In time, the design and color will be dictated by your innate senses. Your choices will become consistent as this now will be part of your identifying style.

When this approach has matured and is consistent, you will have developed a method and nature that is always experimenting. This will be the never-ending growth factor that drives you on. Finding images in the work will foster new ideas for design and color. With this developed style you will paint landscapes, still life's, and a multitude of familiar images. They will manifest in your form and technique without a conscious effort to do so. This will be the point of departure from student to professional, and the time to start a new adventure of exhibiting and sharing.

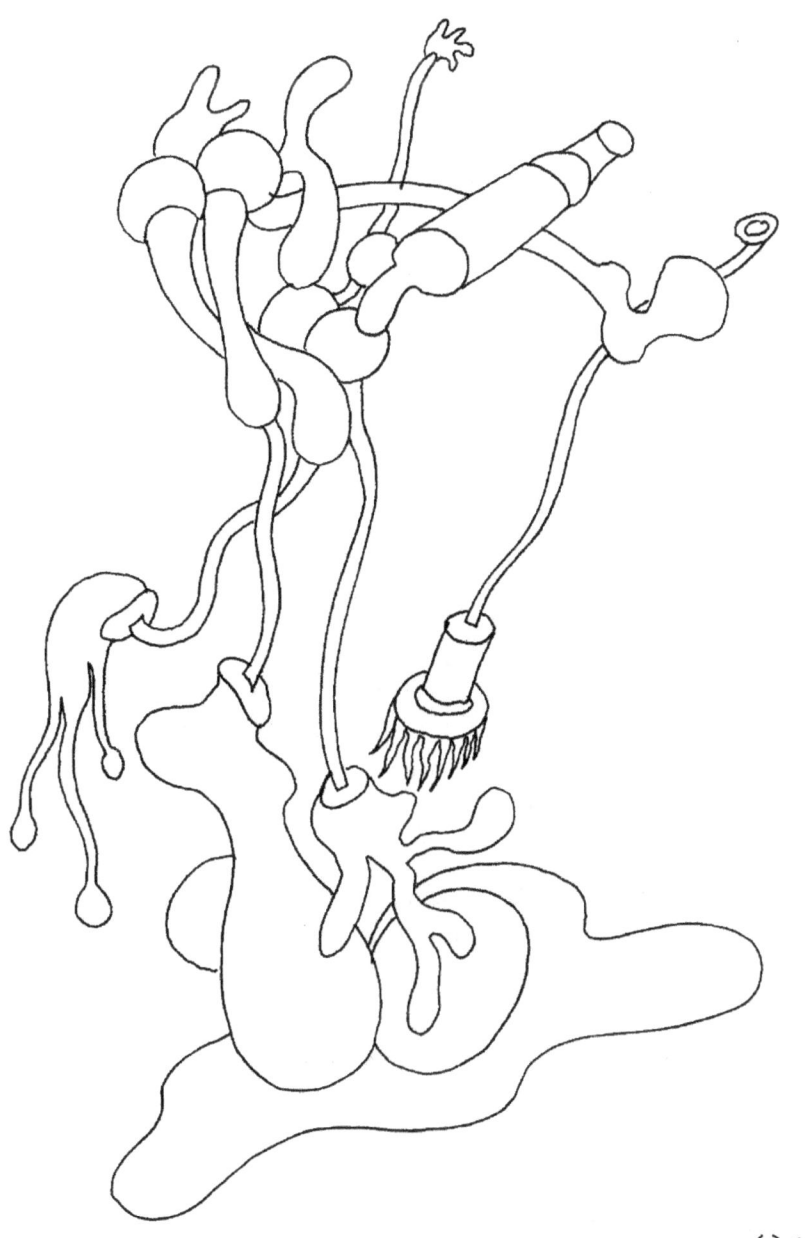

CHAPTER THIRTEEN
The Canvas

VOLUMES AND CONTRASTS

I think it is essential to understand the role of volumes when drawing. Volume(s) are the spaces that define an area and is as important as the shape and intricate design that occupies the adjacent space. The most crucial element of volume is variety. Repetitious volumes make uninteresting compositions. The greater the variety of volumes within a design, the more exciting will be the shapes and designs involved. What then would be the largest shape and the smallest? It would not be prudent for me to try to set forth a formula. This is part of the individual's personal reflection of what is pleasing to the eye. So, keep in mind only that diversity is necessary. Experiment and you will find the combinations that work in your personal world. But remember that overly complicated compositions become more difficult to paint and often defeat the objective.

I have seen very successful paintings with all soft edges and practically no contrast. The palette being lyrical, decorative, and closely related colors in a range of unusual shapes and sizes. This approach is demanding in that you must really ponder the close tonal presentation. It is easily overlooked without some effort in concentration. Contrasts are a way to make one area flow into another without hard lines. Strong contrasts demand attention and combine more elements, always be conscious of the volumes in the drawing and then the contrasts in the painting.

LINE AND DESIGN

I like to sketch my canvas with a pencil, I can erase with a gum eraser if I don't feel the drawing has been effectively transposed. Often, however, when I sketch on the canvas the increased size lends itself to a slightly different outcome. I visualize where it is going, and many times I find that the canvas sketch is better than the original.

When I am excited about a drawing and feel that it will make a successful painting, I draw it many times over so that I know the design and all the possibilities before the translation. I study other drawings to see if there are elements I could incorporate that would enhance the painting. The more times you sketch a design and embellish it, the higher the possibility that the finished work will be successful. Being emotionally tuned in and excited about what elements are utilized will aid in the passion factor. Painting should be a work of passion, but one must remain objective about the design, volume, and contrasts, while the color should be reflective of your personal reactions emotionally. Keep in mind that lines can be visible, hidden, hard, soft and lost.

COLOR, BRUSHES, AND TEXTURE

I gather swatches of color samples from paint stores and make up my own collection on small cardboard squares. I arrange them in several groups of tones: light, medium light, medium, medium dark and dark. I shuffle them using a combination of tones, picking those that excite me. Slowly by playing this game of colors, I pull together a palette for a general idea of where I am going with a particular painting. Just as design must have a theme, so too does color. These individual choices are what defines you in your work.

Color is the joy of painting, embrace it and enjoy the texture and flow onto the canvas. Use pointed sable brushes for the sketch lines that remain visible and soft wide sable brushes for feathering and blending. Sable brushes leave a smooth finish. Bristle brushes leave a texture of the brush stroke depending on the length and stiffness of the brush. Mostly you will use bristle brushes, from a quarter- inch wide to a one-inch size. The bristle brushes should be long and flexible. Use many brushes so that you are not taking the time in the middle of an energy-filled episode to stop and clean them. If you have a stand where the brushes can be set so that they remain with the color that you have last used, you can go back and utilize the brush and color again. A variety of brush stroke and texture add to the interest of the painting, as does the range of color, volumes, and contrast.

All of these elements are the parts of the puzzle, and as you complete more canvases, the various components will become more sophisticated. Remember that both planning and passion are necessary.

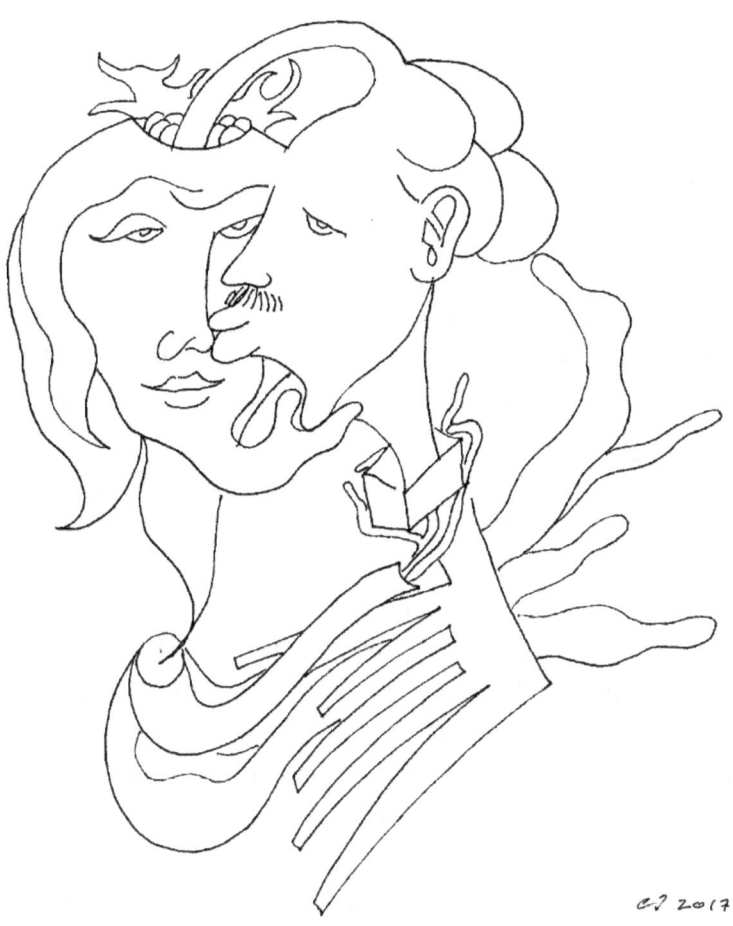

CHAPTER FOURTEEN
The Ghost Images

As the intricacies and style develop and the color begins to have the nuances of the practiced hand, you will find the ghosts and the realities that emerge from your own canvas. You can build upon these images, and their development will add dimension and character to your work. Often the discovery within the work will guide you to investigate similar images, and they will consciously make their way into your mental language of symbols and design. Like lying in bed and seeing images on the plaster ceiling, the picture that you imagine is solely your own. If pointed out, others might share your feelings about the image, but this is a frustrating exercise. Hold them in your own mind and develop them so that they can be shared when the momentum and drive are exhausted and not beforehand.

When you arrive at the point that images emerge where you can build upon them, another transition will begin. After some canvases have developed the ghosts of your psyche, you will start to find your visual investigations leaning toward the discovery of the mysterious and magical in everyday images that surround you in your environment. They are everywhere. Some are abstract, and others are borderline realistic. As your awareness grows, these familiar sights will invade your senses and find their way into your design and color. When your consciousness of creativity has matured, and the work has become a private and exclusive world. You have put yourself in a place of the mind; a magical sphere of imagination that will give you strength, joys, and satisfaction beyond your wildest desires.

There is a story from my life that somewhat illustrates the point of the above. I was a student at the Beaux-Arts Académie in Paris. I considered myself a reasonably accomplished painter. My teacher was a man named Pierre-Jerome, a significant artist of the mid-twentieth century. Pierre looked at my painting and said, "It is a beautiful illustration,; your drawing ability, and your accurate color is impressive. But that is your strength and your weakness."

What he was saying was that I had come so far down the road—artistically—that turning back or changing would be the primary challenge of my growth. Pierre's own work was a very loose and interpretive impressionist style. He distorted his volumes just enough to make them personal, and his color was traditional but consistently different. He was an individual within the framework of Impressionism. How he arrived at this accomplished style, I never knew. But he was in his fifties in 1953, so his influences and mentors were much earlier than mine. (As a note, I visited Pierre in his studio above the Académie de la Grande Chaumière in 1995, and he was still painting very much in the same style.)

Some students were painting in the Atelier at the time, and Pierre asked me to come with him for a moment. An Italian, a very handsome young man, about my age was finishing a large painting. Pierre said he would like us to meet, and introduced me to the painter. He advised me to study the work, and he would discuss it with me later, then walked on to other students. The man was putting the finishing touches to his canvas, and I was aware it was mostly finished. During the next few months, I became friends with the man, and we had many discussions about his work and mine. I was a classic traditional well-trained technician and colorist. He was an outrageous, crazy purveyor of another world. His absolutely wild adventures in paint were fascinating as he was a graduate student and highly regarded by everyone. I liked what I saw, but my first impression was that he must be a very disturbed person to pursue such revolting subjects. He showed me several canvases that first day. I lined them up on the wall and spent an hour trying to fathom what made him tick. I had no intention of letting him influence me with his bizarre images. That evening I appeared at a local nightclub doing a gig with Sidney Bechet, a jazz musician of note. I had a lot of time to just sit around between songs and observe the rowdy crowd in this famous cave on the Rue Colombier. I looked at the scene and imagined what my new friend would do with the subject matter I was viewing. His images were indelible in my mind, and I could not look at anything without translating it to his kind of imaginative interpretation.

Over the next weeks, his work changed my way of observing and recording. I realized that my work was accomplished but not more than many fine painters of an earlier era. I was adding nothing, nor was there anything really individual and personal about it. In later discussions with Pierre, he expressed precisely that! The challenge that I faced and the growth that was to come took many years to come to fruition. I was impaled on the cross of tradition, and the escape route was complicated and arduous. I had not started from the point of imagination and creativity. I had no idea of the abstract and the non-objective and was mightily prejudiced against it as I had been so highly trained. It was many years later that I began to really play with my thoughts and record them as images of a private world. I had enjoyed first my talent and skill, then the praise of an accomplished technician. Then finally I entered my own world, and it became unimportant if anyone understood and praised my work. I was a tower in the desert. I became the dreamer again.

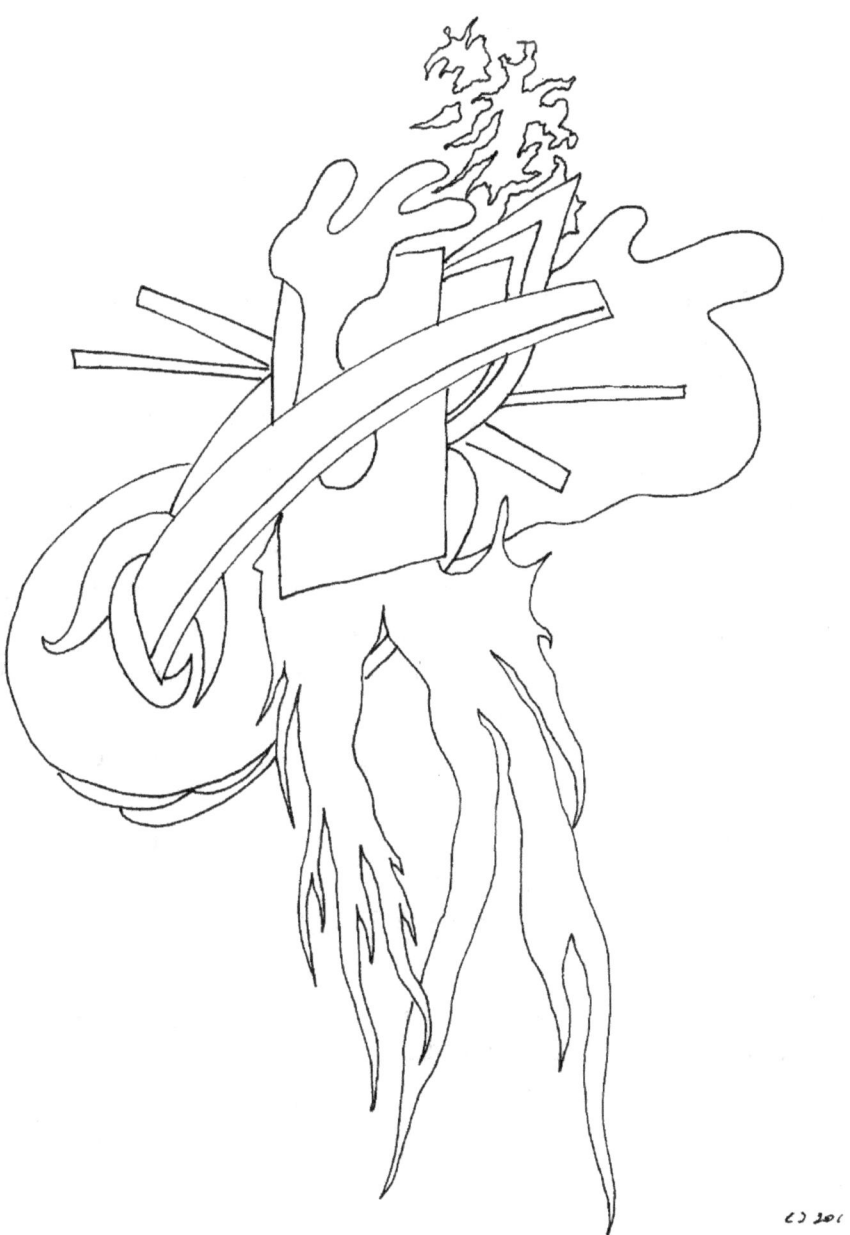

CHAPTER FIFTEEN
The Audience for Your Work

When the work is mature and possesses the elements to capture the viewer, you will have created images and color to appeal to a specific audience.

The past lingers in many ways, in that the galleries still exist and they still promote and sell as they always have. But, their means of contact has changed with the times. The overwhelming portion of their promotion is through social media as opposed to mail, magazines, and periodicals as in the past. This equates to a different procedure and approach for the working artist. In the past, the artist would pursue the gallery, and their future would depend on how successfully the gallery was in promoting and selling their work. The artist would seek some galleries in specific areas so that they had the fullest latitude for success. In the vast majority of cases, the galleries would have limited success in the beginning, and the growth would be slow. Often the gallery would require the artist to pay for his own brochures, openings, and advertising. Because of the competition, this demand was a barrier to the growth of a market for the artist.

In many cases, the gallery would promote primarily friends or close associates, or those who satisfied their own personal taste. Artists with money and a circle of affluent personal friends often had success not based on their talent. Their careers advanced only by social connections and contacts who had a limited understanding of good painting. Also, the dealer in control of the artist's career might have money but insufficient training, experience, and taste. At this point, here in the United States, the whole approach has changed, and the sequence of pursuing the audience has changed to a reversal of the procedure.

The artist of today must build his own following. He creates a website to display his work. Advertising in the art magazines is placed by the artist, with shows listed but the site as the primary contact point. The artist should have a studio where clients can come and view the paintings that have interested them online. Or in many cases, the artist ships the work to the client on approval and the buyer pays the shipping both directions if it is returned. Of course, If the art has no response, he knows it must be developed further.

The skill in building a following is time-consuming and technical, but there are numerous excellent books available for learning. In the overall, it is probably less time than the letter writing, phone calls and shipping of past years. As the personal list grows and the contacts develop across the whole spectrum of possibilities, the sales will increase as well or better than a host of galleries. At the point that the artist has a good following, they then are in demand by the galleries. As they then become a tool for the artist, they—the artists—are in command, and can negotiate from a strong marketing position. It is my opinion that the progression has benefited the artist, as he is now in charge of his own destiny.

The disturbing and sad facts are that the average person has no viewing experience and lacks knowledge of art. Their understanding and point of reference is the photograph. The closer the painting is to a photo, the better they think it is! They are so limited that their taste is dictated by what is cute, tricky, sweet and simple. I call it the candy box approach. So, buckle up and take heart, there will be a very limited audience that will understand anything that is truly creative and imaginative. When you realize that less than five percent of the people have any interest and knowledge about art, you begin to understand the limitations that you must overcome. Study the websites of successful artists, evaluate what elements bring people to them. Make it a part of your program; set aside a few hours for it here and there. But do not let it invade your daily thoughts so that it negatively influences the progression of your artistic endeavors. The audience is there, and you can find them. They those you find—are the intelligentsia and the sophisticated and well worth putting in the effort to interest in your work.

Outdoor exhibits, fairs, and competitive shows are another avenue. Unfortunately, the spectator level is low, and the surrounding presentations may be discouraging. But it is exposure, and there is always the possibility of developing a good contact and educated interest. I have a friend who is a very competent technician. His work is impressive as a representational painter who specializes in underwater scenes. He is not very creative, and much of his work is repetitive, reduced to almost a formula. A client saw these works at an outdoor exhibit, and the man commissioned him to paint an underwater scene mural in his home. The man was a fisherman and had frames and glass put over the mural in his dining room to make it seem as if you were looking into a full wall aquarium. The idea caught on, and several of his friends did similar murals. One thing led to another, and he began to specialize in this style. He devised unique framing and glass applications that over a period of time became very realistic. Thus, a whole career blossomed as a result. His work improved and he moved to Hawaii and confined his realm to this subject matter. One never knows where the path will lead, but do not get stuck in an uncreative and mundane plateau, because so the inspiration and excitement will dissipate.

Keep your identity and artistic identification a firmly in mind, and the audience will find you if they immediately recognize your work. Color combinations can develop and be synthesized into a sophisticated and strong statement—an essential part of your identity. These combinations should expand until you have a reasonable choice to enhance the drawings. I personally have about six or seven combinations that please me and seem to be exciting and rewarding in almost every painting. Although, I am always changing the nuances slightly, and always experimenting with new ideas. The drawings vary with every painting, but the imagery remains with the style that is indelible in my mind. As a result, there is an immediate recognition of my work.

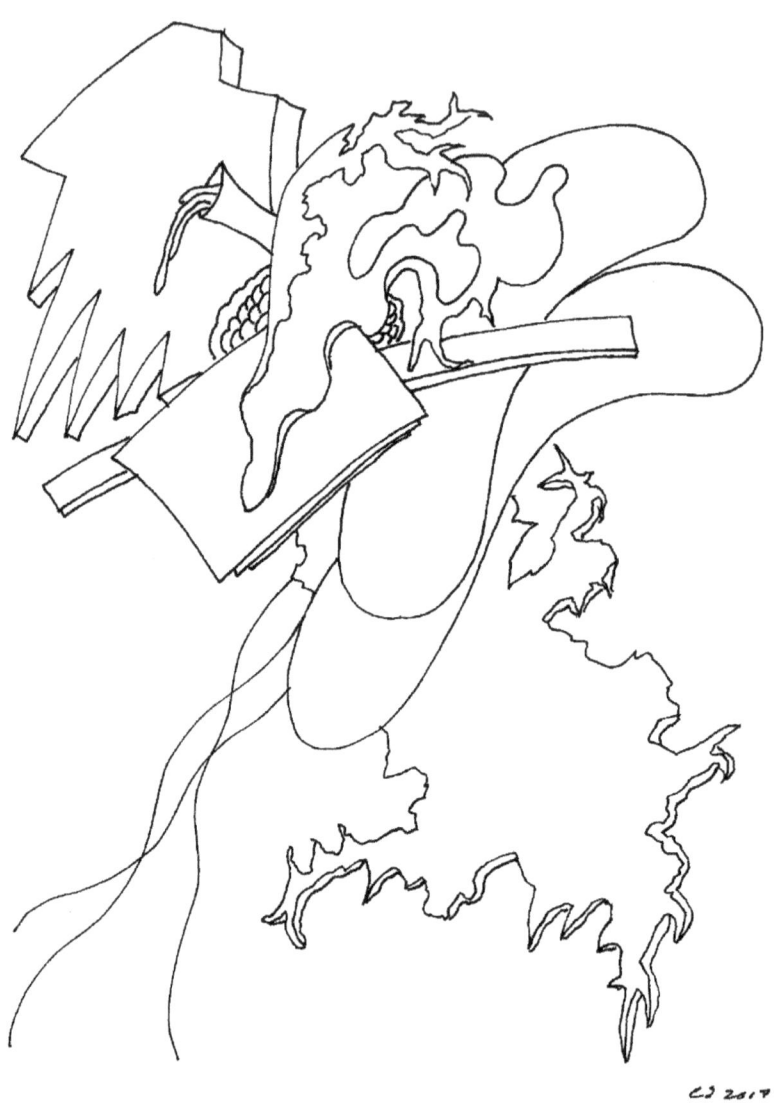

CHAPTER SIXTEEN
Strategy and Promotion

During the study and learning period, when the artist is primarily occupied with the basics, they will either be in the situation of having support financially, or there will be a need to create income. If their drawing and painting skill have real merit, there is possibly an avenue of revenue from that traditional work. But in most cases, this is difficult and discouraging. I believe that a part-time job can be of benefit, either night work when going to school, or several days' employment each week, where a sufficient income can be created to take care of living necessities. If the artist can give themselves three full days of work each week, it is enough. Then they can work without exposure and criticism, and pursue art on their terms.

I have to reemphasize something. The exhibiting of work too soon can be detrimental to growth, as the comments and influence of most dealers and agents are not sophisticated. The artist must be dedicated to the idea that they must find their path and pursue it until it has manifested in an individual mature style and technique. The time required is often a number of years depending on the previous time devoted to the pursuit. I have not seen anyone who arrived at a point that I consider would create a demand for their work in less than five or six years. But, once that level is achieved many knowledgeable dealers will recognize the talent and take on a new and promising artist. The secret is to know when the work has reached a level of unique personal expression. I think it becomes apparent to the artist after a series of successful paintings have maintained the style and consistency. And that style is not forced but is the natural result of a progression of work and experimentation.

The reaction and praise of others are not the keys here. It is the inner understanding that you have produced something new and exciting to the world, a beam of light into a dark corridor that has not seen the light before. You can find many windows in the work of the

Cubists, Expressionists, Surrealists, Futurists, Impressionists, and abstract and non-objective painters. There are voids and points of departure in all of these realms. Understanding the final refinement of a style allows you to build upon those images and make it your own. The foundation will hardly be recognizable with the possibilities that you infuse into the eventual result.

When I think of this oh so important element of personal identification, I am reminded of one particular artist I encountered in my late twenties. He was an outstanding technician, and his drawing and color were sophisticated and thoroughly developed. He produced California landscapes which were colorful and attractive. His show at the Los Angeles Art Association was a great success and Helen Wurdenman, the director and also the critic for the Herald-Tribune newspaper, praised his work and pointed it out to me as the kind of work that could bring me success. The work to me was too traditional, I was already advanced into a personal approach to Impressionism. I decided that the single-source realistic light of the French master Impressionists lacked some magical element and I was experimenting with a dual light source and exaggerating the glare esthetic to compound the drama of a landscape. To go back to the traditional landscape held no interest for me. I felt, even at that time, there was no future in pursuing something that had been done many times before and perfected by so many others. Ken, the artist, had a tremendous ego and exclaimed on several occasions that he was perhaps the best artist living in Los Angeles. Over the next few years, his landscapes failed to continue to sell well. He then turned to figurative works like several other artists that were selling well. For years he jumped from one style to the next, always well executed and professional, but never reaching a sustained audience. His frustrations grew and his lovely wife, who I adored, left him. He fell into a deep depression, and I heard about fifteen years later that he had died. With his exceptional abilities, he never came to grips with his own dreams and symbolism. I don't believe he ever had the strength that could have been developed through his unique personal path. When you harness the images and direction that comes from within, the power of that which exists will guide you.

From a purely commercial point of view, the audience is promoted through recognition of that which is familiar, is comfortable and desired. Why do movie producers pay tremendously high prices for popular stars? Why do you buy the book of an author with which you are familiar? In the world, we pursue that which is familiar and comfortable. Artists as well! But you can be recognizable and remain unique, special and dynamic.

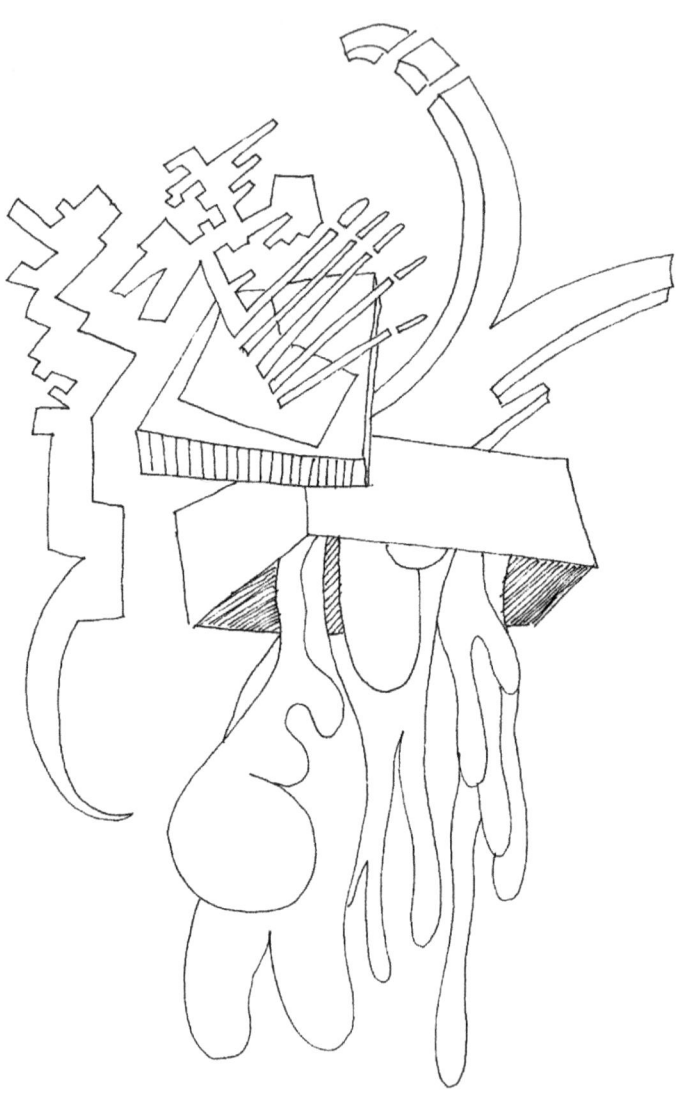

CHAPTER SEVENTEEN
The Future of Our Society

In the last twenty years, the number of galleries has dwindled, while their approach has changed as I have described. But there is a disturbing element present in our society today, and it has very much to do with the future creativity and development of our children. I write this so that each parent can give serious thought to the limitations imposed by the technical advances of our era.

Children today can be hyperactive and spend incredible time on their devices: smartphones, tablets, computers, and electronic games. They join in and participate on multiple websites. They cannot bear to be bored for any period of time. As a result, the term and description of daydreaming is just not in their vocabulary. The time reserved for the mind, and the machinations reserved for dreaming and imaginative thought, is lost. Although the exposure to vast quantities of images and ideas is valuable exposure, unless it is reviewed and contemplated and absorbed in a slow time reference, it cannot be utilized as a stimulus for the imaginative applications that result in creative art.

Every advertisement and the multitude of television and film entertainment is sped up and compressed into momentary flashes to communicate to the audience in quick time. Even the messaging on smartphones is typically in a compressed quick text format. You are compelled to reach your decisions based on bits and pieces, flashes of the whole picture, rarely are we able to receive the story in full and in real time. The frantic pace therefore limits or excludes those without time, inclination or capacity to discern the missing pieces to make it whole. The older people in our society just brush it aside and are unwilling to let the media pace interfere with their wa (harmony). They absorb less but again, it is not an essential part of their lives.

The modern parent must understand the advantages and disadvantages of this spectrum, limit the exposure of the fast and furious, and guide the child into accepting—even learning to enjoy and embrace—moments of inactivity, peace, quiet and contemplation. The sharing of learning of and visiting those temples of the creative giants of the past, will open doors to the young mind and foster creative efforts on a new level. It is not in conflict with the learning of the technology-driven world, but an additional sphere which can encompass a new future and new realizations that lead to exploring depths within ourselves to discover unique talents and abilities.

I can only speak for myself and the close artist friends that I have communicated with about the subject. But, across the board, the serious artists I have known would not sacrifice the rewards they have garnered in their careers for anything that they perceive in the contemporary world. When I have time alone to develop an image that has brought excitement to my whole being, that image as it becomes a finished painting brings me a joy of accomplishment that cannot be replaced in any other way. Every time I see the picture, it brings back the excitement and pleasure from within my mind's vault. There are certain works that I must keep. They are like family, my children and I must keep them protected. They remain with me on this journey (life). The main reason I am building a museum to house my personal collection—that has brought me so much joy, and the individual works that are the landmarks of my career—is that I want others to experience them. I hope continually that there are those who will put it all together and find—from viewing and coming to understand them—the magic of my life.

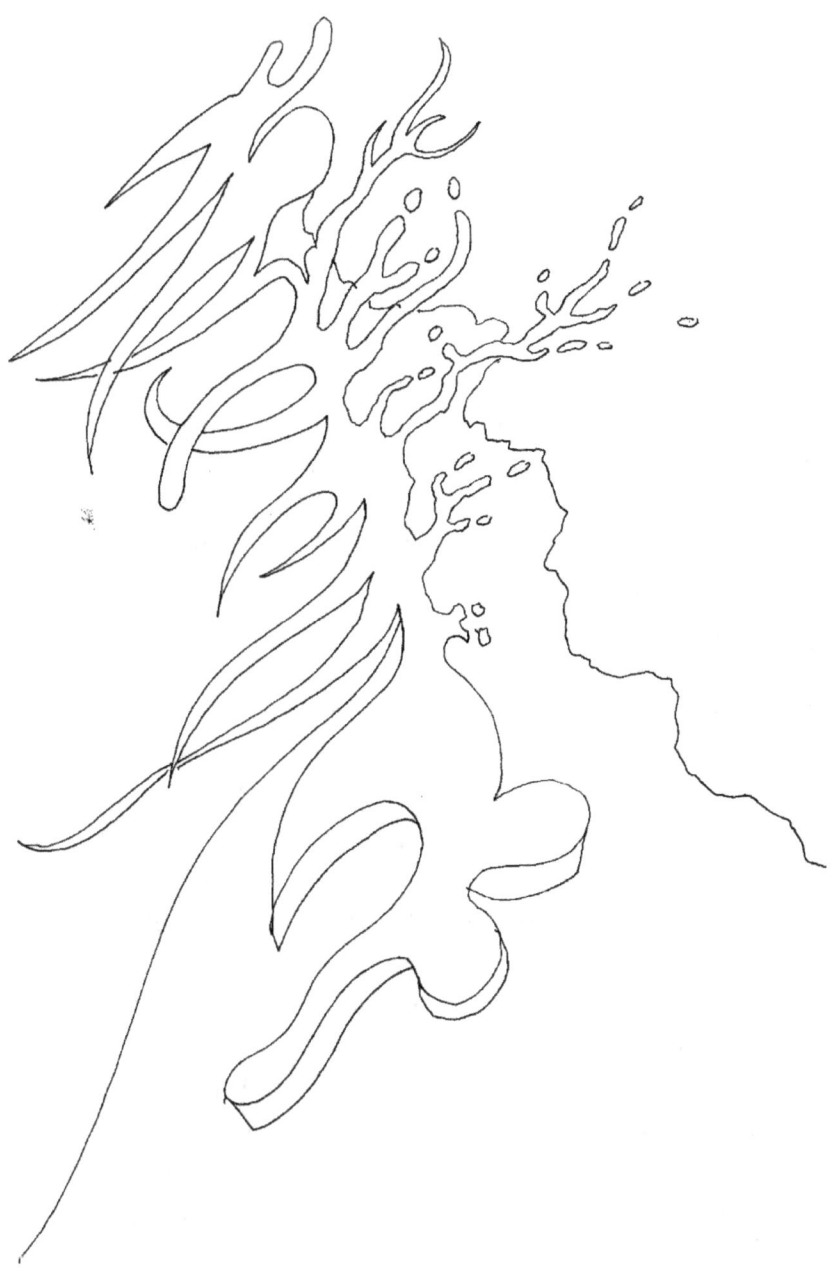

CONCLUSION
The Physiology of Creativity

I have been reluctant to conclude my theories on art with my personal belief in the means in which the nervous system and the mind record the wavelengths and impulses directed by my approach. As I am aware that the scientific community would be highly critical of my personal applications. However, I feel that the understanding of this theory is an aid to the individual who wishes to develop the library of storage which will facilitate the result.

There are patterns in the cortex which record simple sensory experience, a categorizing and filing of the impulses of the eyes, ears, taste, and touch. As we explore and experiment with all aspects of life, the receptors guide and store this information for future recall. But, some of the information is held in limbo and is not immediately filed, a clear path of the impulses is not found. Thus, the mind is working to sort out the correct specificity. This overtime working of electrical impulses is the flash images that we do not control, they come momentarily at unexpected moments, and they manifest in dreams when we are sleeping. Dreams are merely the abstract categorizing of unfiled data. When we explicitly manage the impulses with information that will direct us toward a specific objective, that information then becomes more readily available. The execution and sensory experience compounds the impulses and defines them more clearly in the cortex.

Just the holding of a pencil, pen or brush will trigger channels that feed the imagination. It is only what you put in, that you can take out. The more exaggerated the specific input, the more unique will be the manifestation. In the case of drawing, the design and the expansion and repetition form the progression of neurons coalescing with other wavefronts resulting in the creative sphere that we are pursuing.

ALL OF LIFE HAS A COMMON GENETIC HERITAGE

If you apply derived personal culture and stored sensitizing response to our genetic programming from the first registering of sensation and knowledge to the archive of our emotional foundation and the structure that it has been built upon. You will find the symbols and images embedded deep within, waiting to be discovered. That moving particle is displayed with the language that has been developed by your own emotional responses. There cannot be pure thought, as we have stored elements that subconsciously warp and influence the most conscientious of thinkers. But this is part of the challenge to synthesize our desires and conclusions. We must utilize this personal archive and let it manifest in line and color. There is a common ancestor between all species of life on earth. A small leaf on the Tree of Life. They are few, but they are there, the ones who will share your vision. When you paint for yourself, you will also be painting for them.

ABOUT THE AUTHOR

Christian Title was born in Los Angeles, California in 1932. He has lived most of his life there. In his early years, he lived in Paris for five years, and over the many years he has spent an additional four or five years there, and throughout Europe.

He has traveled in over one hundred countries and lived a total of nearly twenty years in foreign lands. His extensive travel and sailing experiences have been paramount in a life dedicated to art and philosophy, and the gift we've been given to understand the diversity of this planet. It is impossible to record completely a life such as the author's; this book is but the highlights of his desire to live the fullest life possible.

Highly educated, he has authored many articles, essays and contributed much to the field of American Impressionism. His personal paintings and creative work have had considerable recognition, and he continues to contribute to the understanding of the art world.

He has committed to his desert community and is currently planning his legacy to the art world. An art center and museum housing his personal collection of American Impressionist paintings, his personal works, and space for international exhibits. The Center will have studios to fulfill the desires of aspiring artists, with an extensive art library for reference.

Other books by Christian Title: *Climbed the Hill* (the artist's autobiography) and *Christian's World* (three hundred drawings from the artist).

www.ingramcontent.com/pod-product-compliance
Lightning Source LLC
Chambersburg PA
CBHW051328220526
45468CB00004B/1541